AF511645

Brick by Brick

"ALL THAT WE ARE IS THE RESULT
OF WHAT WE HAVE THOUGHT,
THE MIND IS EVERYTHING.
WHAT WE THINK, WE BECOME."

Buddha

THE SMILE OF A LIFE WELL LIVED
Sushil as he is today

Brick by Brick

the life and times of

SUSHIL ANSAL

SHOWCASE
Roli Books

All rights are reserved. No part of this publication may be transmitted or reproduced in any form or by any means without prior permission from the publisher.

SHOWCASE
A Roli Books imprint for titles sponsored by individuals or organizations.
© Roli Books, 2011
Published in India by Roli Books Pvt. Ltd.
M-75, Greater Kailash II Market
New Delhi 110 048, India.
Phone: ++91.11.4068 2000
Fax: ++91.11.2921 7185
Email: info@rolibooks.com
Website: www.rolibooks.com

ISBN: 978-81-7436-824-9

Text: Ashok Malik
Photographs: Saibal Das
Editor: Shalini Krishan
Design: Sneha Pamneja

Printed and bound in India

ACKNOWLEDGEMENTS

This book would not have been possible without the commitment and effort of some special people in the life of Sushil Ansal. In particular, he would like to thank the following:

His wife, companion and sheet-anchor: Kusum Ansal

His children: Archana and Vipin Luthra, Alpana and Rahul Kirloskar, Sheetal and Pranav Ansal

His larger family: Indira Puri and Meenakshi Varma [his sisters], Vinod Saigal [Kusum's brother], Rajinder Miglani [Sheetal's father]

His friends: K.P. Singh, Ramesh Chandra, Ashok Kapur, Swaraj Kaushal, Prabhu Chawla

The book team: Pramod Kapoor, Priya Kapoor, Sneha Pamneja, Saibal Das, Ashok Malik

FOUR PASSIONS

Sushil is devoted to his wife, his work, travel and golf

CONTENTS

IN LIEU OF A PREFACE

Between seed and tree, there is a long journey, for which the seed requires proper care. But for Sushil, there was no guiding icon or guru to nurture him. He only had his own compulsive inquisitiveness, and the desire to learn. He explored the vast world of books and some, like *How to Win Friends and Influence People* by Dale Carnegie and *Positive Thinking* by Normal Vincent Peale, came to his rescue. These books helped sharpen his understanding of the complexities of life and how to deal with them.

He grew up in a middle-class family with financial and emotional difficulties surrounding him, but managed to maintain a distance from envy and greed, which so often smoulder in an early life of troubles and insecurities. Rather, Sushil developed the unusual power for positive thinking. It helped him maintain his equilibrium and keep his cool during problems and crises. This trait has never gone away.

All his life Sushil has taken up professional and personal challenges and overcome them with nothing more than the simplicity of action and an amazing inner strength. As Abraham Lincoln once said, "it is not the years in your life that count. It is the life in your years." That is Sushil's motto.

Kusum Ansal

PHASE ONE

LAYING THE FOUNDATION

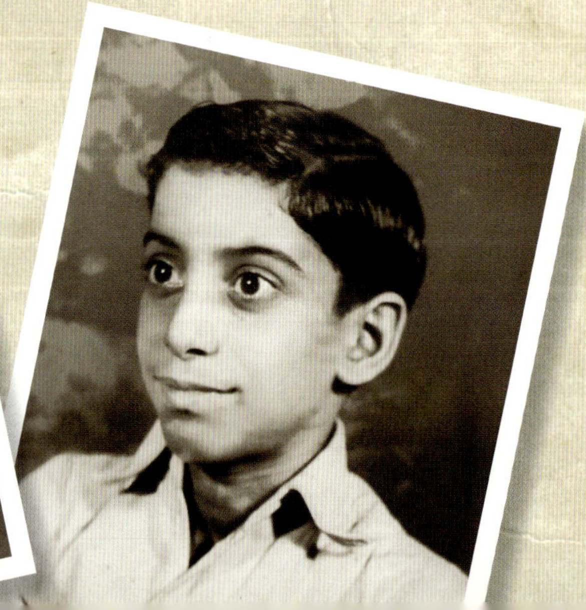

If you lived in north India, you wouldn't ever have had a good word to say about April in Delhi. The searing heat of summer, the baking earth and scorching winds make life decidedly uncomfortable. Physical torment is only complemented by mental fatigue and feelings of listlessness. There is very little to look forward to; the following month promises to be worse still, and the monsoon is weeks away.

April, as it happens, is also Delhi University's month of choice for its examinations. It was on a typical hot afternoon in this month in 1960 when the third-year students of St Stephen's College walked out of the hall, having submitted the last of their answer sheets. The ordeal was over, the weather excruciating and the future a gamble. Yet, for the moment, it was time to relax. The chatter and laughter of the students grew louder as they ambled down to the gate. Picnics were planned, as were holidays, or even an immediate trip to the movies. Other discussed applying overseas for higher studies or – that holy grail of generations of Stephanians – taking the Civil Services examination.

One of the students, a tall and gangly but obviously physically fit young man of 21, was part of the conversation and yet away from it. He was game for a movie but more fixed on the future course of his life. His father wanted him to study for the Civil Services examination, but he had decided he would join the family contracting business instead, and seek his destiny among bricks and in the labour and ordered excitement of construction sites. This was inevitable, he told himself; it was the route he had chosen and, sooner or later, he would embark on it. The choice had not been smooth. His father felt the contracting business was not a very dignified one and left its practitioners vulnerable to the whims of junior engineers in the government. Yet, the son found the entire process of building engaging and creative.

Facing page
THOSE WERE THE DAYS
Sushil as a young man

As he walked out of the University and moved towards the road, the young man was a little surprised. Right outside he saw a familiar white Austin and sitting in the back was his father. The older man got out of the car, and having confirmed that the examination was over, told his son that he had brought him a suitcase with his clothes and a few essentials. He was going to drive him to Hapur, about two hours away, to a construction site that he was to supervise. He had better get into the car quickly because they had a long way to go and there were instructions to be given, which he would receive en route.

The young man jumped into the car, without so much as looking back at his friends who were still deciding which film to see, and drove into the future. Sushil Ansal's career had begun.

The man who had inaugurated the career in so abrupt a manner was Chiranji Lal Ansal, clearly a martinet and, at 54, already a veteran of the contracting business. Sushil's father – Bawji as he was addressed by immediate family – was a moderately rich man who had come a long way from his humble beginnings without, however, losing his moorings. Chiranji Lal was not a native of Delhi. He was born in the small village of Kahma (in Tehsil Nawashahr, two kilometres from freedom fighter Bhagat Singh's villlage) in Punjab's Jalandhar district in 1906. He began life as a clerk in the Northern Railways. When the new imperial city of New Delhi was built, the Northern Railways headquarters moved here, and so did Chiranji Lal, along with his wife and two daughters. Amid the vast avenues of the new city, something happened to him: he began to dream big.

Chiranji Lal was plain bored of the drudgery of his job. He felt he was built for other things, maybe even intellectual pursuits. He had been a good student at school and had a sharp memory. His felicity with Urdu and Persian was exceptional, as was his interest in mathematics. Along with a friend, Soni, he started a small business, the Teachers Tutorial Corporation (TTC), to train teachers for schools.

The Ansals lived in a two-room flat on Panchkuin Road. In 1939, Chiranji Lal's family expanded with the arrival of his first son. Sushil was not born in a hospital but at the Jain temple on Hanuman Road, near Connaught Place. The story goes that his mother, Suraj Kumari, was being taken to the hospital from Panchkuin Road but the baby would not wait. Suraj Kumari, who was about three years younger than her husband and

Preceding page, top
THE NURTURERS
Sushil's partents Chiranji Lal and Suraj Kumari

Preceding page, below
WEDDING TIME
Sushil with Kusum

Facing page
PRIME OF YOUTH
As Sushil was setting out in life

Top
SOURCE OF INSPIRATION
Sushil's father, Chiranji Lal

came from a family in Rajpur village near the city of Hoshiarpur village, went into labour early and had to be taken to a shelter at the Jain temple. The baby was clearly self-willed and determined about his own time table, a bit like his father!

Proof of Chiranji Lal's determination came soon enough. Soni had been training to become a lawyer and, on getting his degree, decided to give up the teaching business to go full-time into law. Chiranji Lal now had a choice before him – withdraw from TTC as well, or resign from the Railways and become an educational entrepreneur. With a wife and three children to feed, it was not an easy decision. Yet, Chiranji Lal took the risk. His colleagues and seniors thought he was crazy to walk away from a government job and its perks and security – but his mind was made up. He resigned from the Railway Department in November 1941, fourteen years after he had joined it as a young man at the age of 22.

Chiranji Lal resolved to expand TTC into a proper school. He began running a school on Panchkuin Road, near his residence, and later moved it to a rented site on what is today Feroze Shah Road. Ironically, Sushil's current home is a few yards from the former location of his father's school, but that is a story for later. Chiranji Lal took on a new partner for the running of the school. He also befriended S. Saran, the owner of a fairly well-established contracting company. Saran was looking for an honest but hard-working person to help him grow his business. He found Chiranji Lal suitable and, in 1942, offered him an assignment.

Initially reluctant, but attracted by the idea of earning for his family and learning a new skill himself, Chiranji Lal agreed. It proved to be a blessing. A few years later, his partner in the education venture betrayed his faith and cheated him of his school. Chiranji Lal was emotionally broken, but not financially damaged. So successful had he been in the contracting business that Saran had already elevated him from employee to a minor co-shareholder and partner with a ten per cent stake in the business.

For a good decade, Chiranji Lal worked in Saran's company Engineering and Contracting Syndicate. By 1952, Chiranji Lal was restless again and eager to break out on his own. Independence had come in 1947. The government of free India was expanding its seat in New Delhi. The city was growing and so was the bureaucracy. New homes and offices were needed. The influx of Punjabi refugees was also expanding the housing market. Chiranji Lal felt this was as good a moment as any to seek a slice

FAMILY ELDERS
(right to left) Chiranji Lal, Om Prakash, Surendra Kumar, Desraj, C.L. Puri, Baldev Krishna, Gurdasram and Sushil

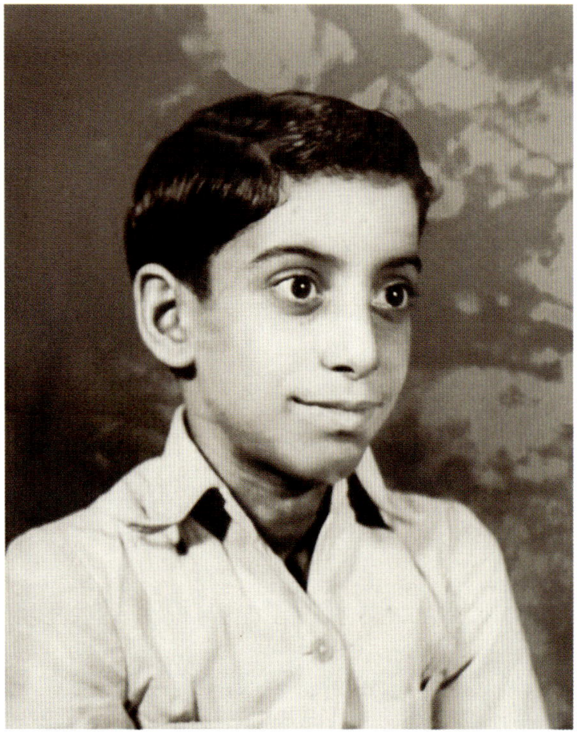

of the contracting business. As such, he set up C. Lyal and Company – Lyal being the anglicised version of Lal – and soon was registered as a first-class contractor with the Military Engineering Services (MES), the Central Public Works Department (CPWD) and, finally, the Indian Railways.

C. Lyal and Company executed government contracts, building bungalows on Pandara Road and government quarters in Vinay Nagar. The contract that gave Chiranji Lal particular satisfaction entailed building part of Baroda House, headquarters of the Northern Railways, where he had once worked! His life had turned a full circle.

As he had expanded his horizons and nurtured his ambitions, Chiranji Lal's family had also grown. When he was four, Sushil and his family had moved to a large ground-floor apartment in a building called Madras House in Daryaganj. There were four rooms, a kitchen and an open courtyard. Sushil remembers it as "relatively spacious accommodation". It was so spacious that Chiranji Lal, who had an obsession with healthy eating and fresh food, kept buffaloes here for the daily supply of milk.

The Daryaganj experience lasted only eight years, and in 1953 the family was to move again. However, the Madras House years shaped Sushil's earliest memories. He used to walk to the Cambridge School. Shy, with a slight stammer, he tried to avoid school and "had to be dragged there" by his maternal uncle, Gurdas Ram. That affliction was soon overcome, and lifelong bonds were forged at Cambridge School. Dinesh Mathur, now one of Delhi's leading lawyers, was his classmate. "We used to bunk classes and play table tennis in Dinesh's large family mansion," recalls Sushil. There were less pleasant memories as well – principal A.C. Deb once barred Sushil from an elocution contest on the grounds that he was a Punjabi and his pronunciation couldn't possibly be correct! This left an impression on Sushil who still cannot understand how a school principal could entertain such prejudice.

The iconic event that shaped Daryanganj, Delhi and, really, India in the period the Ansals lived in Madras House was, of course, the Partition

SCHOOL DAYS
Sushil was an inquisitive child

of India. As a young boy, Sushil encountered violence on the streets and saw the character and geography of his area changing. Muslim neighbours now migrated to the "part behind Golcha cinema". Refugees from Lahore and Rawalpindi brought their own flavour. They were Punjabis like the Ansals but from other parts of Punjab. The Ansal family traces its origin to a small village near Nawashahar (Jalandhar district) in eastern Punjab, not the big cities of western Punjab that are today in Pakistan.

Nobody realised it then but the Punjabi influx was to transform Delhi society forever. A quiet town of bureaucrats and a fading Muslim gentry, the city acquired a new energy – and perhaps even a survivor's aggression – with the post-Partition refugee communities seeking to rebuild their lives and, indirectly, their new city's fortune. In the decades to come, as Delhi's Punjabis came of age and deepened their emotional and other investments in the city, they were to be among Sushil's prized customers and clients. Yet all this was well in the future; for the moment, the Ansals were migrating once again, this time southwards.

In 1953, Chiranji Lal moved his family to his own house at 57 Jor Bagh, now in some of the most valuable real estate in India but then a young neighbourhood. It was a large, 575-square-yard plot of land, and Chiranji Lal built a two-storey house, renting out the ground floor and moving in with his family to the first floor.

Sushil's father was an adamant Congress man and, in those early years of independence, saw politics and public life as part of the nation-building process. His Jor Bagh house was often a Congress election office and host to several political figures of the day. In particular, Chiranji Lal became close to Sucheta Kriplani and I.K. Gujral, later the prime minister of India. Chiranji Lal was also elected, from Aliganj and Lodhi Road constituencies, to the Electoral College of Delhi. As a young boy, Sushil remembers canvassing and working for his father's election.

Sushil also had to change schools and was admitted to the fledgling Delhi Public School on Mathura Road. "There were no buildings, no structure," he remembers, "the building only started to come up after I finished school. We had our classes in tents." It was a very different Delhi. The days were silent and the nights still. Often the garden in Jor Bagh was visited by jackals from the nearby Lodhi Gardens. Sushil has very vivid memories of this house. His two sisters were married from there. In 1962, he brought his bride, Kusum, there. He remembers his younger brothers,

Gopal and Deepak, growing up there; and his three children were born while Kusum and he lived with the joint family in Jor Bagh.

Those early years were tough but rewarding. Sushil remembers his mother as a lady of limited formal education but great earthy wisdom. "She could easily run the house within the limited means that my father was able to provide," he says. Suraj Kumari was deeply religious and passed on this quality to Sushil. She was excessively fond of her first son and tended to pamper him, family confidants feel, because she had lost two boys earlier, one in childbirth and the other soon after.

As the first son, Sushil was always conscious of his father's expectations. While C. Lyal and Company was doing well, Chiranji Lal was not keen on his son becoming a contractor. "This can be a humiliating business," he told Sushil, "you have to run after junior engineers and petty officials for routine clearances and to get payments that are due to you. Minor permissions can be delayed; there is a lot of corruption and dependence on the government. You are not treated with respect." Especially after Sushil got into St Stephen's College, Chiranji Lal urged him to take the Civil Services examination and attempt to join the Indian Administrative Service (IAS).

Sushil's interest did not lie in bureaucracy, however. As a schoolboy, he had accompanied his father to construction sites, and been fascinated. There was a certain "act of creativity" that left the young boy in awe – "brick and mortar being mixed, forming different shapes". As he sat with his books – Chiranji Lal was very clear that Sushil had to come along with his books – the idea of a calling had begun to form in his mind.

Chiranji Lal was still not convinced. He continued to point Sushil towards the Civil Services. The clinching counter-argument came one day when Sushil gave him the example of Sir Shobha Singh, the father of the writer Khushwant Singh and one of the biggest contractors who had helped Edwin Lutyens and Herbert Baker fashion the Delhi of their imagination. "Sir Shobha was still alive," Sushil says, "and he was an icon in the construction business. The name inspired me, and his family was much respected". He cited other examples, such as that of Tirath Ram Ahuja, a contractor who had built beautiful embassies in Delhi's diplomatic enclave, Chanakyapuri, and Gammons India, which undertook big civil engineering contracts and earned a name. "'So why should we shy away from contracting?' I asked my father," says Sushil.

SPIRITUAL INFLUENCE
Sushil's mother Suraj Kumari was an emotional anchor

St. Stephen's College, Delhi

Name Sushil Ansal

Class III-Yr. Econ. Hons.

Year of admission 1957

Principal's Signature

Renewal

Year	Class	Subject	Initials

Signature of Student

Chiranji Lal decided to test him out. In 1957, in the six months between his final school examinations and entering college, Sushil was given charge of constructing a house on 6th Link Road, near Jangpura, not far from the Jor Bagh residence. It wasn't smooth sailing. An accident occurred during construction when part of the roof caved in. Nobody was injured but the incident was a setback and Sushil was left shaken.

He carried out an assessment and realised the structural design was at fault. The reinforcement that the steel bars provided was inadequate for them to be load bearers for the span of the barsati room, resulting in the caving in of the roof. In his recommendation, Sushil wrote that every structural design, for every project, must compulsorily undergo a third-party audit. This is now standard procedure in any Ansal project. In a sense, it was Sushil's first business innovation – fairly remarkable for a teenaged non-engineer.

College life was fun, and engaging. Sushil enrolled for Economics Honours and N.K. Singh, later Finance Secretary to the Government of India and now a Member of the Rajya Sabha and Arun Shourie, the popular journalist turned politician, were his classmates and close friends. Sushil used to go to College by public bus. Three decades later he ensured his son, Pranav, went to Delhi University by bus as well.

Memories of his college days are still sharp. Every year, irrespective of how busy he is, he makes it a point to attend the annual St Stephen's old

COLLEGE CACHET:
Sushil's St Stephen's identity card remains a proud possession

students' dinner. Here he looks forward to meeting old mates like K. Natwar Singh, former foreign minister, Surendra Singh, former cabinet secretary, Vishnu Bhagwan, former Chief Secretary of Haryana, S.Y. Qureishi, now the Chief Election Commissioner of India and Montek Singh Ahluwalia, the deputy chair of the Planning Commission.

At St Stephen's, Sushil found the sports arena dominated by tennis and cricket. He introduced basketball, a sport he had come to love while in school. Encouraged by a friendly sports teacher, Nag, he built a College basketball team and in the first year helped it win the Delhi University Inter College Championship. The following year, he captained the Delhi University team at the inter-university championships in Calcutta and lost to Punjab University who won the Championship. What drew him to basketball? "It taught me team building, anticipating the moves of team colleagues and moving fast." To this day, Sushil recommends basketball as a team-building exercise.

Even at Delhi Public School, Sushil made long-standing friendships on the sports field. Among the people he is still in touch with are Narpinder Khanna, a big Delhi based exporter, and Vishnu Bahadur, who has recently retired from the IAS.

Ashok Kapur, now a management consultant based in the city of Princeton, was among Sushil's closest friends at Delhi Public School and at Delhi University. After graduation, he left for the University of North Carolina for his MBA, becoming a professor before branching out on his own. Thereafter, for a quarter-century, the two friends were not in contact. In 1984, Ashok was visiting India and staying with his brother Jagmohan in Delhi's Panchsheel Park. One evening he went for a walk and found Sushil's name outside a house – Sushil and Kusum had moved into their own Panchsheel Park home in 1973, as 57 Jor Bagh was beginning to be too small for their growing family. His curiosity provoked, Ashok walked in and inquired if "this was the same Sushil Ansal?" It was, but he wasn't home. "We met a few hours later, and it was like old times again."

In the past 25 years, Ashok and Sushil have grown much closer. Ashok knows and understands Sushil as few do. "I can identify characteristics from his schooldays that establish continuity," Ashok says. "He was always curious: 'Not what is it, but why is it?' Sushil was a very keen mountaineer and he organised a trek to Pindari glacier in high school. At 12,000 feet, he was so curious about plants and animals at that altitude.

Even when discussing management theories with me, there is a genuine desire to understand: 'Why are things the way they are? Do they apply to what I'm doing?' There's a constant desire to learn".

This curiosity and sense of adventure were very much with Sushil that day in the summer of 1960 as he drove down to Hapur, where his father's company was constructing grain godowns and silos. His introduction to the harsh realities of life couldn't have been more immediate. The days were blazing and the nights excruciating. Sushil slept under a tin roof – covered with grass to cool the room – often without his shirt on. Hapur was far removed from Delhi. Recreation meant a post-dinner walk to the railway station two kilometres away to read books at the A.H. Wheeler stall there, and "just look at the faces of people on the platform". It was a tough experience, but those eight months made a man out of him.

Om Prakash and Baldev Krishna were both partners in a contracting business in Punjab. Chiranji Lal had had a few dealings with them and liked them. He got his daughters, Sheila and Leela, married to them and made them part of the family. In the early 1960s, Om Prakash and Baldev Krishna had got the contract to build aeroplane hangars and the runway at the Chandigarh airport. After Hapur, Sushil was sent to train under his brothers-in-law in Chandigarh.

Next Chiranji Lal sent Sushil to Amritsar. He had bid for a contract to build a military cantonment with the sole intention of making Sushil in charge of the project. Here, Sushil developed a friendship with Sudarshan Goyal of Messrs Pyarelal Hari Singh, a reputed contracting firm that was building another part of the cantonment. Sudarshan being his senior in the profession, Sushil took a lot of guidance from him. He became an early mentor. The association continues to this day. Sudarshan and his two sons have strong personal and business ties with Sushil and are contractors for some Ansals projects.

While in Amritsar, Sushil received a message from his father one day asking him to pick up a friend, Surendra Saigal, from the railway station. Saigal was the owner of Tiger Locks, a big manufacturing company in Aligarh. A stalwart individual, he had studied abroad at a time when few Indians did so, and counted the country's elite as among his friends. Feroze Gandhi had been his roommate at Allahabad University.

His visit to Amritsar had another purpose. He had met Chiranji Lal and the two men had got along well, deciding that Kusum, Saigal's daughter, could be the right match for Sushil. Not that Sushil knew any of this when he reached the railway station, only to realise that he was too late and that "Mr Saigal had already left". Deeply embarrassed, he traced Saigal and went to meet him, apologising for the morning's confusion. It was a short meeting and Saigal asked him about his work. Sushil answered as honestly as he could, not realising this was an interview of a different kind. Saigal then returned home to tell Kusum that he had found the right match for her.

At the time, the Ansals were still middle-class folk. The Saigals had a higher social standing. Kusum was a writer with an MA degree. She was the granddaughter of a man who had studied in Britain, among the first Indians to do so. Sushil was only a graduate and had no legacy fall back on, only a future to build. Yet, Saigal instinctively knew he was the right choice. "I suppose my father saw Sushil minus his background," Kusum says today, when asked about how Surendra Saigal made that critical choice. "He judged Sushil extremely well. He obviously saw something in him that the ordinary eye would miss. He made up his mind in an instant".

CENTRE OF ATTENTION
Sushil with his father and father-in-law at his wedding in Aligarh in 1962

Facing Page
MR AND MRS ANSAL
February 28, 1962

Left
AT THE WEDDING
With Kusum's brothers Vinod and Pramod

Below
TASTING THE WEDDING CAKE
Kusum and Sushil at their wedding

After completing the Amritsar project, Sushil came back to Delhi to help build the erstwhile Ranjit Hotel, where a modern office complex, built for Anil Ambani, stands now. Soon it was time for his wedding.

The wedding took place on February 28, 1962, amidst extraordinary arrangements. A school was rented to accommodate the guests and cooks were requisitioned from as far away as Delhi. A sit-down dinner for about six hundred people was the highlight of the evening, a result of the organizational capacities and hospitality of Surendra Saigal and Tiger Locks. Those who attended the wedding remembered it for a long time. It was an elaborate affair, as Kusum's father was a well known figure in Aligarh and throughout Uttar Pradesh. The *barat* drove down from Delhi and was received at two locations en route, first at Bulandshahr, on the banks of a picturesque canal, and then in the *haveli* of the Nawab of Chattari, a good friend of the Saigal family.

STILL IN A DAZE
Kusum and Sushil in their early marraige days

Following the wedding, Kusum and Sushil went for a short honeymoon to the mountains of Darjeeling before he ended up once more in the plains. In 1962, China attacked India and the resulting military setback was a psychological blow to the young nation. Military and infrastructure preparedness had to be ramped up on an emergency basis. Seven new airports were to be built. One of these was in Amausi, then on the outskirts of Lucknow, and the contract was awarded to C. Lyal and Company.

Today, this is the Chaudhary Charan Singh Airport and not too far from a township built by the Ansal Group. In 1962, it was a very remote location. Logistics were difficult. Sand had to be brought in from Bundi in Rajasthan and gravel from Jhansi in Uttar Pradesh. Much of it arrived on slow-moving rail wagons. Sushil's father and his partners worked hard on this project and the company completed it on time, winning praise from the Defence Minister at the time.

They also went on to successfully execute challenging projects of national importance, like the construction of a part of the Narmada Canal in Gujarat, the Thoubal multi-purpose project in Manipur, infrastructure development for Tehri Dam Project in Uttar Pradesh and the Baner Hydroelectric Project in Himachal Pradesh.

A three-year (1962-65) stint in Gorakhpur followed for Sushil, as C. Lyal and Company was constructing a fertiliser factory there. Bordering Nepal and deep in eastern region of Uttar Pradesh, Gorakhpur was also where Sushil and Kusum set up their first home. Archana, their first daughter, had been born in 1963. Immediately after she arrived, Sushil left for Gorakhpur, leaving Kusum with a newborn baby and a large joint family to look after.

When Alpana was born two years later in 1965, Kusum protested that they needed to live together as a family. Sushil took the three women

in his life to Gorakhpur and they spent about a year there, enjoying their private moments as a foursome and going for excursions in the nearby forests, a time which Kusum invoked in her memoir, *As I Am* (1997).

By 1966, the fertiliser factory was completed and the family returned to Delhi, though Sushil kept going back to Gorakhpur to claim bills and wind up the work. It was in this period, in 1967, that his son Pranav was born. It was a new beginning in more than one way. The Delhi property market was readying for a life-altering change. A central business district was being planned by the government. Sushil, restless as ever, smelt a chance. He was getting bored of the contracting business, and saw the opportunity before many others did of moving into real estate development. It was a natural progression – a backward integration in the modern management jargon.

Yet, he faced a compelling question. Real estate needed initial investment to buy land. Where was this money going to come from?

DAYS OF INNOCENCE
The honeymoon in Darjeeling

AS THE YEARS PASS

Sushil and Kusum stroll in the garden of their home, Vishranti, in the heart of Lutyens' Delhi

PHASE TWO

REACHING FOR THE TOP

ansal API

Building lifestyles since 1967

In the years after World War I, the British conceptualized and built the city of New Delhi, seeing the new capital of India as an inherently government town. They made allowance for a legislative building, the viceroy's residence, and facilities for the military brass as well as places of work and residence for civil servants and their families. Commercial infrastructure was confined to markets, the grandest and most elegant of which was the circular Connaught Place, modelled after the Royal Crescent in the English city of Bath.

The reasons for this were not hard to gauge. The British saw New Delhi as an administrative location with a small population, not as a busy business city. In their view, business and trade would still be conducted in Bombay and Calcutta, thriving centres of commerce for two centuries. It was felt that New Delhi, with no access to a port, was too far inland to be useful to businessmen. Nor was it deemed necessary for British trading companies and mercantile firms to set up offices and establishments in New Delhi except where necessary to serve the local (or north Indian) market.

When they began constructing New Delhi, the British felt they were shaping a capital for an empire and a way of doing business that would last forever. That New Delhi would soon be the seat of an independent country, one in which the government controlled the levers of economic power, did not strike them. Neither could they guess that a city deep in the hinterland, far removed from the sea, could someday emerge as a business hub, given changes in technology and the nature of the economy.

Within a decade of Independence, India's new rulers – and New Delhi's new masters – realised that the initial plans for the city were obsolete. In 1957, Parliament passed the Delhi Development Act. The Delhi Development Authority (DDA) came into being and began work

Preceding page, left
A GAME CHANGER
A.N. Jha, the then Lieutenant Governor, inaugurates Akashdeep on April 15, 1969. This was New Delhi's first commercial high-rise building

Preceding page, centre
THE CENTRE-PIECE
Ansal Bhawan houses Ansal API's headquarters

Preceding page, right
SEEKING COUNSEL
Sushil in a discussion with his father-in-law, Surendra Saigal

on the "Master Plan for Delhi". The Master Plan was released in 1961. It focused on the vast gaps in residential and commercial requirements that had emerged in the city.

The period since Partition had seen Delhi's population balloon, especially with the arrival of refugees from West Punjab. The government of India had also expanded as public servants from across the country had moved to the capital. Most importantly, many new offices had been opened by big Indian companies, multinational corporations (MNCs) and multilateral agencies. The search for quality office space was growing by the day.

Up to this point, the Chandni Chowk-Kari Baoli-Sadar Bazar area was the principal central business district (CBD) in the city. It was recognised as being congested and inadequate. The Master Plan envisaged changing the land-use pattern in the area around Connaught Place and redeveloping it into a CBD, complete with New Delhi's first high-rise buildings. "To meet the increasing demand of commercial space in central areas," the Master Plan document read, "it is recommended that the Connaught Place commercial area be extended up to Keeling Road [today's Tolstoy Marg] ... It is also proposed to have 15 district shopping centres to decentralise commercial activity and to make each division of the city self-contained."

The town planners laid stress on vertical growth, permitting the construction of multi-storeyed buildings in some areas. Initially, there was no height restriction for commercial buildings, and in theory, they could go as high as the builder wanted. The only restriction was that the floor space index (FSI) was limited to 400. For residential buildings, eight floors and an FSI of 150 were deemed sufficient.

As with so much else in India, these words and this sentiment took time to become reality. The Master Plan's implementation hinged on the putting together of zoning plans that would detail the exact use – residential, commercial, institutional and so on – of each zone/property and the mix to be permitted in different areas. The Connaught Place extension zoning plan (Zone 3) arrived only in 1967.

By the mid-1960s, Sushil had begun to nudge his father in the direction of real estate development. When the Master Plan was released and in the discussion and consultation that preceded it, he sensed that there were opportunities coming. The Ansals had experience in contracting and knew the construction end of the business. As such, Sushil saw moving into full-scale property development as a natural corollary.

As early as 1963 – in anticipation of the finalisation of the zoning plan – Sushil had persuaded his father and father-in-law, Surendra Saigal, to put down an advance for the purchase of a 2,056-square-yard plot on 26A Barakhmaba Road. A bungalow belonging to an old Delhi family, the Guptas, stood here. In 1965, the price was renegotiated, as the Guptas now wanted more. Finally, a small tailor's shop in the premises proved an obstacle. The tailor tenant refused to leave and had to be taken to court. By 1966, the Ansals had made the full payment of about Rs. 4.5 lakh, and the Gupta bungalow was ready for demolition.

Even for a successful contracting firm, it was, at that point, a massive risk. Essentially, Sushil had paid for a property without any idea of when the zoning plan, and subsequently, sanction to construct would arrive. He needed capital as well and this came from his father-in-law. In fact, the property was bought by a new partnership entity: Chiranji Lal, Surendra Kumar and Others.

The wait was relatively short. In 1967, the zoning plans were luckily finalized. The following year in 1968, Sushil's company got permission to build the first office high-rise in Delhi. This was a historic event in Delhi's vertical growth. For Sushil, it was a leap in the dark. Even so, he had his reasons for being confident. He knew the city and its property market better than most people. His informal market surveys had also been encouraging. He had identified several layers of potential clients – buyers for the office space he would construct.

"Banks were expanding, liaison and marketing offices of big corporate houses needed quality offices," he says, looking back, "Chandni Chowk and Old Delhi businessmen wanted to move to more organised locations." In the absence of a CBD, misuse and misrepresentation were rampant. Many MNCs and foreign business representatives were living in rented accommodation in tiny neighbourhoods such as Jor Bagh and Sunder Nagar and their residences were doubling as offices. This was illegal and Sushil assessed they would welcome the prospect of a modern and legal office complex – Akashdeep.

Also, there didn't seem to be much competition around. In the years after Independence, the big property developer in Delhi was DLF. It had gone into promoting colonies like Greater Kailash, Hauz Khas

GOPALDAS

CHANGING DELHI'S SKYLINE
Ansal API is credited with its creation

AKASH DEEP
IN

and Model Town, essentially dividing a very large tract of land into small plots, taking care of internal infrastructure but not building homes. Kailash Nath & Associates was the other major company with similar ideas. It started building Himalaya House, on Kasturba Gandhi Marg, around the same time as the foundation was being laid for Akashdeep. However, Akashdeep came up first.

Despite offering his logic, Sushil could not easily convince his prospective customers. "Friends remained sceptical and warned me I was taking a big gamble," he remembers, "but my gut feeling was this was a risk worth taking. Basically, I was driving the idea".

What *was* the idea? Akashdeep was designed as a twelve-storeyed structure, with 70,000 square feet of built-up area (including the basement). Each floor had eight units, a mix of two sizes: 450 square feet and 750 square feet. Compared to today's sizes, these units seem small, and indeed they were. "Our assessment was companies were looking to buy or rent liaison offices, or chambers for lawyers and other professionals," says Sushil, "each unit would seat 7 to 12 people. Smaller units would also be affordable for buyers". If users required more space, it was possible to combine numerous smaller office units. "We found," says Sushil, "that the investing class was different from the end-users."

The conservative approach was also dictated by the fact that selling partitioned office spaces was a new concept for Delhi, which was not used to the culture of high-rise building. Bookings for Akashdeep opened at Rs 75 a square foot and gradually climbed to Rs 100. Some of the higher floors went for a discounted price: Rs 70 a square foot. Sales were slow. "We hardly sold one office unit in a week," says Sushil of the early months. Each sale had him buying three boxes of sweets from Bengali Market: "One for the buyer, one for colleagues at my office. And one to take home in celebration!" Sales were mostly done to old business associates and friends. They bought because they had faith in Sushil and his family. None of the early customers was a stranger willing to trust an unknown builder.

Neither it was easy to clarify and explain the idea of joint ownership of common areas. Many prospective buyers turned up and asked for their portion of the 2,056-square-yard plot. They were rather astonished that there was no equivalent of a single plot on offer. An individual buyer's area of the 2,056 square yards could not be defined

AKASHDEEP
Delhi's first high-rise (1969)

by bounds. Passage to office units on the same floor; common areas and their maintenance; elevators; security: these were shared assets and responsibilities and would require regular and uninterrupted cooperation with one's neighbours. Yet, this was no cooperative movement among the economically less prosperous. It was commercial co-ownership. This new concept did take lot of time and energy to be accepted by the prospective purchasers of office space.

It was also taking place in a legal vacuum. Akashdeep came up in 1969 and possession was offered thirteen months from start of construction. This actually preceded the Delhi Apartment Ownership Act. Mutation remained a problem, as the plot had no single buyer to whom the Ansals could transfer ownership. Finally, it was decided that each unit would be governed by a tripartite agreement between the flat buyer, the Ansals and the Land and Development Office (L&DO) of the Government of Delhi.

As it happens this tripartite agreement has not been executed to this day, 41 years after Akashdeep came into being. The situation is similar in all the other multi-storeyed office complexes in the Connaught Place region – primarily on Barakhamba Road, Kasturba Gandhi Marg, Tolstoy Marg and Hailey Road – and the legal lacuna has been allowed to persist.

The New Delhi Muncipal Council (NDMC) raised house tax bills in the name of the developer/builder (the Ansals) for the entire building. This was unfair since it was difficult to collect the house tax from the individual owners and deposit it with the NDMC. It took a few years of persuasion and numerous representations before NDMC agreed, in the early 1970s, to raise house tax bills in the name of individual apartment owners. In a sense, government agencies were fine with the notion of individual ownership when it came to collecting taxes, but not when it came to granting legal ownership under the Transfer of Immovable Properties Act, 1882.

There were similar problems with the Income Tax Department. It would assess the "notional rental income" from the building and seek taxes from the developer. It did this in the absence of the title for each flat not being transferred to the individual purchaser. However, the cheques and rental income being received by each individual purchaser were also being taxed, as per his individual returns. This amounted to double taxation and was legally untenable. The matter was ultimately resolved by the Supreme Court of India, in favour of the developers.

All this notwithstanding, Delhi's first skyscraper – at twelve floors, the word can only be used advisedly – was an imposing structure. It was the subject of much curiosity when inaugurated by A.N. Jha, the then Lieutenant Governor on April 15, 1969. It had been designed by Chatterjee & Polk. To ensure it was a financial success for investors, the Ansals had to resort to a degree of hand-holding. "We had created a dedicated renting department," says Sushil, "that took charge of renting out Akashdeep on behalf of the buyers. Often units were merged to create bigger offices. The lease rate was Rs 3–5 per square foot per month". The returns were generous. In two years, unit owners would recover their money. This first building was sold on the carpet area basis and not super area as the practice is today.

The impressive rentals acted as a trigger. The re-sale value of Akashdeep units shot up. Some initial buyers decided to sell immediately, pocket the profit and move on. Having tasted blood, they turned to Sushil and began asking him about his next project. Spurred by the success of the Akashdeep experiment, Sushil had three projects lined up, all within walking distance of his dream debut.

The first of these was Ashadeep, a residential complex. The name was derived from Kusum's mother's name, Asha Rani. Each 1,800-square-foot apartment would have three bedrooms and a servant room. Ashadeep was located at 9 Hailey Road. This was an old house owned by the Maharani Sitaba Sahiba of Palitana, widow of Maharaja Bahadur Singhji of Palitana. On the evening that Sushil paid the final instalment and got the sale deed in the name of Ansal & Saigal Properties Pvt. Ltd, he received news that his company was likely to be served a notice from the government of Delhi asking it to hand over the property in two days as the administration wanted to requisition it to house its offices. The logic was that the house had been lying unoccupied for a few years.

The previous owner had an inkling of this situation but had not warned Sushil. He was left carrying the can. As soon as he read the notice, Sushil consulted his lawyer Mr. Ravinder Narain of M/s Dadachanji & Company. He was advised that there was only one solution: demolishing the building, which was already in a dilapidated

condition, overnight. There would then be no building to requisition! Accordingly, 100 people were called in from various construction sites and work continued through the night and by dawn the structure had been weakened sufficiently to make it uninhabitable. Sushil was present every minute and even ate at the community kitchen that had been set up for the workers

The drama continued. In the morning, the notice arrived. "At about lunch time," adds Sushil, "we sent a telegram to the Acquisition Department saying the building was not fit for human habitation and that requisition made no sense. We got a response the following evening, with a demand that the government be allowed to inspect the building immediately." By then the old building was on its last legs. Sushil was safe.

Ashadeep was the first multi-storeyed residential complex in New Delhi. The concept of living in apartments was novel for Delhi residents and the initial buyers were largely outsiders: migrants from Bombay or companies that saw logic in investing in a guest house in central Delhi. The eleven floors and 44 apartments of Ashadeep were ready in fifteen

ASHADEEP

Built on Hailey Road, this was New Delhi's first multi-storey residential complex built in 1970

months, by early 1971. With a swimming pool and tennis courts thrown in, the building was the talk of the town. Each apartment had been sold for around Rs. 1.20 lakhs. Today they are valued at about Rs 6 crore each. The flats were sold on the basis of covered area – an evolution from carpet area – but still not super area, as is the practice now.

Though Ashadeep went off smoothly, it was clear that the real money and profit margins lay in commercial projects. Sushil rolled the dice again – launching two projects, both much larger than Akashdeep and coming up bang opposite each other. Surya Kiran, 19 Kasturba Gandhi Marg, was completed in 1972 on 1.5 acres of land. Sushil got lucky here as the company that owned the plot, M/s Ferro Alloys, had gone into liquidation. It had been sued by creditors and the matter was in court. Sushil was advised to make a bid directly in court and carry a bank draft with him. "Fortunately, the Court accepted our offer as sufficient to pay off the creditors. In half an hour we had the property," says Sushil, still incredulous after all these years. "It was my fastest purchase. We named it Surya Kiran to honour my mother, Suraj Kumari." It was the first building with a triple basement for parking in the Connaught Place extension area.

However, it was Ansal Bhawan, 16 Kasturba Gandhi Marg, completed in 1973, that turned the Delhi property market. In 1970, Sushil had bought the 1.5 acre plot from a leading advocate of the city, Mr Wanchoo. This was a gigantic project. It entailed a massive 330,000 square feet of built-up area. Along with Surya Kiran, it would release some 600,000 square feet of office space at more or less one go. Was the market deep enough to absorb this expansion? The answer would make or break Sushil.

The new building was to be named Ansal Bhawan. Since it would bear the family signature, Sushil was keen to have a design that was both aesthetically beautiful and functional. A design competition followed and the work of Chander Kukreja of C.P. Kukreja and Associates was finally selected.

Bookings for Ansal Bhawan opened in 1973. The sale price had been set in the Rs 100-160 per square foot bracket, depending on the floor. On the morning bookings commenced, there was a clamour outside the Ansal office. "It was like the first day of a big film," recalls

ansal API
ANSAL BHAWAN

Sushil, "within an hour we sold all we had planned for the first day and put a sign 'Sold out for the Day.' We had to ask remaining prospective buyers to come back the next day". In a week, half the building had been sold. The Ansals retained some of the floors for their corporate headquarters, releasing whatever remained gradually and increasing the sale price progressively. They eventually raised their rates to Rs 200 per square foot.

The scramble for Connaught Place had begun. Delhi's mad property rush had hit the fast lane. Sushil realised it was wise not to be in a hurry to sell an entire building. There were greater profits to be made by selling gradually and increasing rates as the construction progressed.

Seeing the buyers making hefty profits, Sushil introduced the concept of transfer charges from the seller (if an original buyer re-sold to another). Initially there was resistance but the concept is now accepted trade practice.

Ansal Bhawan was completed in 1975 and Sushil moved his office there, making it the seat of his fledgling empire. The two rooms they had been operating from in Akashdeep were now clearly inadequate for a company that was beginning to dominate the Delhi market and had become synonymous with the redevelopment of Connaught Place and its environs. Investor interest in the Ansals began to gallop and Ansal innovations and products began to become part of the property business. "Our launch prices went up to Rs 300 a square foot," Sushil points out, "we began selling units even before plans had been sanctioned. These were the first ever pre-sanction sales." This innovation by Sushil got accepted by the market due to the company's record of delivering projects on time and honouring business commitments, whether verbal or in writing.

An indication of the market's trust in Sushil and of his personal brand equity came in 1976. DCM (then Delhi Cloth Mills) wanted to sell its 1.5 acre property on 22 Kasturba Gandhi Marg. Today, this is the location of Antriksh Bhawan but in the mid-1970s it was an old house with Dr. A.K. Sen, at the time one of Delhi's best known doctors, as tenant. The DCM patriarchs, Lala Bharat Ram and Lala Charat Ram had entrusted their nephew, Bansi Dhar, with negotiating the sale. Sushil knew Bansi Dhar socially and went to see him. A price of Rs 40 lakh was agreed, but there was one strict condition: Bansi Dhar wanted almost

ANSAL BHAWAN
Sushil's headquarters on Kasturba Gandhi Marg, built in 1975

half the sum in 48 hours. Sushil nodded, the two men shook hands and the deal was done.

Despite his spontaneous response, Sushil was worried. Rs 20 lakh wasn't small change. "Simply put," he confesses, "I didn't have anything close to the amount." He went back to office and called his brokers and his known investors. He told them he was planning an exciting new project but that he couldn't disclose the details – no address, rate, size of office unit, nothing. However, he was open to advance bookings, on payment of Rs 2 lakh a flat. "This was not so much a commitment to buy," Sushil says, "as a guarantee of being offered the right of refusal. If the investor didn't like the commercial sale terms of the project after it was formally announced, the Rs 2 lakh would be returned with interest. The only security offered for their money was my word."

It was one of Sushil's trademark gambles, and also a test of his credibility in the market. In the end, it took only 90 minutes of working the phones and making persuasive calls. Solely on the basis of his verbal proposal, a series of brokers and investors agreed to send in the money. By the next morning, ten individuals had deposited a total of Rs 20 lakh. Bansi Dhar had his money and Sushil got access to prime property. More meaningfully, he realised just how much goodwill his name generated. It was a humbling experience.

Antriksh Bhawan became more than just another project. It had a lot of emotions embedded in its foundations. It was a mammoth complex – 450,000 square feet of space became available when it opened its gates in 1979. "We wanted to create a landmark," says Sushil, "and crowned Antriksh Bhawan with Delhi's first revolving restaurant."

For Sushil, business and relationships have always formed an intricate band. It happened in the making of Antriksh Bhawan as well. Right after paying DCM, he went to meet Dr. Sen, who was now his tenant. The doctor wanted a few months to move out, as his new residence was not yet ready. "It was our first meeting," Sushil says, "even though my daughter Alpana had been born in Dr Sen's Nursing Home."

The two men hit it off and Dr. Sen confided he was heavily in debt. Dr Sen's Nursing Home was a showpiece medical institution in Delhi, a private facility with state-of-the-art equipment. Dr. Sen

ANTRIKSH BHAWAN

Another Ansal API building on Kasturba Gandhi Marg, built in 1979. Its crowning glory was Parikrama, Delhi's first and only revolving restaurant

Antriksh
Bhawan
ansal API

had taken loans to set up his hospital but the good doctor was, alas, not a businessman. He told Sushil he wanted to shut down the hospital, located on Bahadur Shah Zafar Marg, liquidate its assets and repay his creditors. He asked Sushil for advice.

Sushil stepped in with Rs 80 lakh and bought Dr Sen's Nursing Home in 1979. The building was remodelled into an office complex and in eight months the units were made available to buyers. The customers were mainly tax practitioners and advocates as the building was walking distance from ITO (Income Tax Office). The building was named Hans Bhawan, in honour of Sushil's paternal grandfather. The name, like those of other Ansal buildings, was given by Kusum, the litterateur in the family.

Meanwhile, the scorching pace had to be maintained. The block between the Outer Circle of Connaught Place and Tolstoy Marg became Ansal territory. Sushil eyed a strategically located corner plot at the juncture of Tolstoy Marg and Kasturba Gandhi Marg: 14 Kasturba Gandhi Marg. The owner, Bhawani Shankar, came from well to do family and was himself living in the bungalow. It took a lot of persuasion to get him to agree to collaboration with the Ansals. Their credible track record helped. Chander Kukreja created a remarkable design for the building, which came to be called Ambadeep. The 23-storyed structure is the tallest building in Delhi in the private sector (taller than the historic Qutab Minar) and was later recognized as among the most notable buildings of the twentieth century by Sir Banister Flight Fletcher, the British architectural historian.

The next mission was a challenging one. Sushil wished to amalgamate and develop three adjoining plots – 15-17 Tolstoy Marg and 1 Tolstoy Lane, located just behind the other two – and build one composite complex. However, the ownership was in the hands of three different families or sets of individuals. How could he handle this?

Above
UP ABOVE
A panaromic view of Delhi from the heights of Parikrama, in Antriksh Bhawan

Facing page
AMBADEEP
At 84.10 metres high, Ambadeep is taller than Delhi's historic Qutub Minar

In 1978, Sushil came to know that H.R. Malhotra, father of Omi Malhotra – who is today a golfing friend of Sushil's – was interested in disposing of his property at 15 Tolstoy Marg. Malhotra had negotiated with another builder but Sushil approached him, bettered the offer and sealed the deal. Now it was the turn of 17 Tolstoy Marg, which was owned by two brothers, Brahm Swaroop Sood and Ramesh Chandra Sood. 1 Tolstoy Lane had three owners: Shakuntala Patel, Sunita Sharma and N.K. Sood. All owners had different views and requirements. With his trademark diplomatic skills, Suhsil eventually won over all the stakeholders. A joint venture development agreement was agreed upon in 1983 and Tolstoy House was completed in 1988 after buying a lane which was running between the 15 and 17 Tolstoy properties.

The family behind the popular Delhi jewellers, Kapoor di Hatti, was looking for a developer to help with its property on 19 Barakhamba Road. There was a family dispute amongst the Kapoors but luckily the Ansals had been buying jewellery from them for years. Sushil therefore knew the members of the Kapoor family and was trusted by them. An eighteen-storey building, with a built up area of 225000 square feet, came up on this plot in 1987. It was an imposing structure, designed by Bharadwaj and Bharadwaj Associates, with a structural glazed façade. It was named Indraprakash after the matriarch of the Kapoor family.

Meanwhile Sushil had not forgotten the success of Ashadeep, where prices had skyrocketed. He decided to build three more

residential complexes, negotiating to buy two plots on 5 Hailey Road (Gauri Sadan) and then 1 Hailey Road (Upasana). Another building Dhawan Deep, came up on 6 Jantar Mantar Road.

One of Sushil competitors in high rise constructions in Delhi at that time was the upcoming M/s Skipper Builders headed by Shri Tejwinder Singh. Sushil admired Tejwinder's aggression and his meteoric rise in the real estate sector, finding in him a tough competitor. In one prestigious auction for a plot at Jhandewalan, Sushil sensed that competition may lead to unviable bidding. He rang up Sardar Inderjit Singh, the legendary Chairman of Punjab & Sind Bank to mediate with Tejwinder Singh and avoid competition, ensuring a collaborative bid. In the meeting at Inderjit's house, "I suggested that we could save crores of rupees by joining hands and avoiding competitive biding by buying plot in a neutral company's name and then dividing the complex in two equal halves or have some other collaborative arrangement to our mutual convenience," says Sushil. However, despite Inderjit Singh's advice, Tejwinder Singh refused and said he was adamant to own the project at any cost. As a result, the competitive bidding went high, beyond any sensible calculations. Tejwinder Singh came out victorious. Unfortunately, the unworkable price proved to be a disaster. This inappropriate bid started Tejwinder Singh's downfall and ultimately his company went into liquidation, with several types of litigations against him and his company. "One lesson I learnt was never to do business to satisfy one's ego," ruminates Sushil. "The Skippers' going into liquidation affected the image of the real estate industry. I feel sad till today for Tejwinder Singh; though a competitor, he is a friend."

PRAKASH DEEP
Another massive office complex that the Ansals built on Tolstoy Marg

Another interesting auction was of a five-acre hotel plot in Nehru Place. The bidding was very tense. Mr. C.L. Verma of Continental Construction, Mr. Amrit Singh Bhandari of Bhandari Builders and the Ansals were in the race. Some sense prevailed and the three on the spot decided to join hands together rather than indulge in mad bidding. "Jagdish Sood approached me to see if he could also join as a fourth partner. We agreed and after buying the prestigious plot, I reached home. Kusum and my mother were unhappy: they asked why I am entering into the hotel business where a lot of chicken and cow meat is served, gambling takes place, etc. All my explaining did not help but I never wanted to annoy my mother and wife. I preferred to buy peace at home. A few weeks later I surrendered our share in favour of Sood & Company," relates Sushil. Later on Mr. Bhandari and Mr. Verma also sold their shares to Sood, who built today's Intercontinental Eros Hotel. "It took me a few years to convince my family to allow us to enter the hospitality business. It was only in the year 2002 that we successfully built Marriot Welcome hotel in Saket District Centre," says Sushil.

The piece de resistance had to wait till the mid-1980s: Statesman House. The flagship Delhi property of the *Statesman* newspaper was a coveted corner site, opening out to both Barakhamba Road and the Outer Circle of Connaught Place. Plans to break down the old structure and build anew had been discussed since the 1970s but the chosen partner had defaulted. Sushil was keen to step in. He spoke to C.R. Irani, managing director of the company, and was invited to lunch at Statesman House in Calcutta.

Irani was a clever man. He had few cards but he played his hand well. "He served me a lavish Parsi lunch," remembers Sushil, "really laid it on, and dazzled me with the grandeur and history of the newspaper." It was a complex deal. The company was in a mess; debts had to be settled and workers to be paid from the proceeds of the sale. The agreement gave the Ansals immediate possession of half the plot. The *Statesman* authorities retained the other half and were only allowed to hand it over to the Ansals after they had used the money given to them – in lieu of the first half of the property – to pay their workers and settle with the banks and union.

Today, of course, only the name "Statesman House" remains and only a small portion of the building is occupied by the newspaper. It

STATESMAN HOUSE
OXFORD

is one of the jewels in the Ansal crown – Sushil's last major project in the Connaught Place area, completed in 1993. Sushil took a personal interest before approving an appropriate design by the Bombay-based architects Gherze Eastern Private Ltd. who gave a curvature to the building "to keep it in harmony with the circular design of Connaught Place."

In a sense, Statesman House was an exception. It came up in a time when India had grown more prosperous and people began to see aesthetic appeal as an essential ingredient, not an indulgence. Sushil's earlier projects in Connaught Place had flowed from another philosophy: functionality. Top architects had been engaged, but had been constricted as buyers and tenants wanted an emphasis on economy. "For instance," expands Sushil, "there was no glass frontage as this was energy consuming and air-conditioner intensive." Nobody had time for such luxuries; these were not designed as swanky offices of globalizing businesses in a post-liberalisation India, but were nonetheless landmarks of their times.

Nevertheless, Sushil made every effort to make his buildings aesthetically pleasing and contemporary. For example, Akashdeep, Ashadeep and Ansal Bhawan have impressive murals on ceramic and glass tiles in the foyer and façade. This idea came to Sushil when an acquaintance brought his deaf and mute but extremeley talented son to him and sought help. Ravindran, the young boy, was obviously an outstanding mural sculpturist and Sushil decided to experiment with his work. The result was a great success, as the murals instantly bear testimony.

In 2010, Connaught Place is an overcrowded urban nightmare. Much of this is the fault of city planners and municipal bodies. How does Sushil look back at the changing character of the area he knew so well as a boy growing up in Delhi? The leafy bungalows have gone, leaving behind only the sameness of densely-populated office blocks. "It was a necessity," he says, "a central business district had to be created. If I hadn't been there, somebody else would have taken the initiative." He built almost fifty per cent of the high rise buildings in the Connaught Place Extension area and, in a a sense, changed the skyline of Delhi.

Yet, for a man who is so particular about minute details and neatness, Sushil is disappointed at the general impression Connaught Place creates. He says he is happy at the refurbishing of the area, restoring grandeur and making signage uniform. Nevertheless, it hurts that users

AESTHETIC APPEAL
Statesman House was carefully designed to integrate Connaught Place's curvature

are not house proud. “Maintenance of a complex depends on those who use it, their work ethic and sense of pride,” he argues, “if users don’t pay upkeep charges on time, if they care for their own offices but not common spaces, the general look will suffer.”

What also disappoints him is the attitude of government agencies, which shamelessly exploit Connaught Place but gave very little in return. Visitors to cities like Hong Kong marvel at the intensive walkway network there – all-weather overhead corridors that connect one building to another and take pedestrians off the road. The CBD in the Connaught Place extension area had provision for just this in the early 1970s. Developers paid charges to NDMC to build elevated walkways and link all those buildings on Barakhamba Road, Kasturba Gandhi Marg and Tolstoy Marg. It was never done. "This has congested the area and made it a nightmare for pedestrians,” Sushil says. “With elevated walkways they could have crossed from building to building without having to run past the speeding cars.”

The Master Plan of 1961 had also spoken of district centres, in addition to the CBD. Sushil was a pioneer in these areas as well, helping provide a spread of commercial space for the Delhi sprawl. The first District Centre was Nehru Place, with DDA beginning auction in 1972. “We bought two plots,” Sushil notes, “numbers 90 and 94. It was a rocky area and snake infested. Labourers were scared.” Friends discouraged Sushil from bidding so far away in South Delhi. They feared nobody would shift to the future Nehru Place, desolate as the location was. However, Sushil could visualize the growing pressure and increasing demand on commercial space and sensed the opportunity in providing such space at cheap, affordable rates. Connaught Place Extension and the CBD had become out of reach for many.

This was the high noon of Indian socialism. Along with the economy, urban planning also operated on command-control principles. At Nehru Place, the architectural façade was left to the DDA and only the internal layout to the developer. That is why the buildings tend to appear uniform, and uniformly dull, from the outside. There were other spectacular shortcomings. The DDA decided the norm would be one car parking slot for every 1,000 square feet of built-up space. Today the norm is to plan for two cars in 1,000 square feet, if not more.

Crucially, the responsibility for building car parks was taken over by the DDA and developers were allowed to use basements as storage spaces. "The planners did not have the foresight," Sushil laments, "and did not correctly assess the need for car parking." The DDA and the Municipal bodies were very tardy with their part of the bargain. Pedestrian walkways, water supply and fire services arrived in Nehru Place well after the Ansal's and other developers had handed over office units for occupation. Today the upkeep of Nehru Place is appalling. "We are insulting our great statesman Jawaharlal Nehru," Suhsil laments, "by naming such a poorly maintained district centre after him."

Even so, the demand-supply gap was considerable in a Delhi that was consuming quality office space faster than it was being created. "Nehru Place picked up very fast," Sushil remembers, "in 1975 or so we began selling property here at Rs 200-300 a square foot. The first occupants were banks and public sector companies." By this time, the re-sale price of Ansal-built office units in the Connaught Place region had climbed to Rs 2,000 a square foot. Seeing the initial success, other builders started bidding in open auctions and Nehru Place become a thriving building complex. The DDA filled its coffers.

Of the sixty buildings in Nehru Place, the Ansals built ten, becoming the single largest developer. By the early 1980s, Nehru Place was becoming saturated. So the DDA began auctioning plots at Rajendra Place (where Sushil built three high-rises) and Bhikaiji Cama Place (where the Ansals built two). Finally, the Ansals also moved into the Janakpuri and Laxmi Nagar district centres, in the west and east of the city. This helped in the decentralization of commercial activities in Delhi and made it a city of multiple CBDs.

Sushil took the initiative in every district centre. In fact Jagmohan, Vice Chairman of the DDA between 1971 and 1977, was a very good administrator and Sushil and he often exchanged notes on the development of district centres. Sushil holds Jagmohan in high esteem for his drive, foresight and enthusiasm in improving Delhi.

Unfortunately, the Master Plan had not accounted for cultural centres, good restaurants, shopping malls or even movie theatres. Nehru Place, to cite an example, is completely deserted after office hours, with only Paras cinema drawing small crowds. Sushil noted this lacuna fairly early but there was almost nothing he could do about it. He was unable to design and build entire neighbourhoods or townships. That was still the government's prerogative. He could only shake his head at missed opportunities. Despite appealing to the government through business associations of which he was the spokesman, such as the Federation of Chamber of Commerce and Industry (FICCI), the PHD Chamber of Commerce and Industry (PHDCCI) and the Rajdhani Promoters & Builders Association, he couldn't get his suggestions heard.

It was the feeling that the potential of the leisure economy was being not just underestimated but thwarted by the city planners that got Sushil to experiment with forays into hospitality and entertainment complexes. In 1992, the first hotel plot was tendered as part of the Saket district centre and Sushil walked away with the prize. To fund his hotel project, the giant Japanese company, Itochu, became an equity partner. During construction some shares were sold to ITC Hotels Ltd. who with their tremendous experience and professional input commissioned the hotel. This hotel is today the ITC Sheraton, the Ansals having sold out a few years ago. In the process Sushil developed good professional relations with Y.C. Deveshwar, the dynamic chairman of ITC Ltd. and Habib-ur-Rehman, the earlier managing director of ITC Hotels Ltd. a connoisseur and himself a great cook.

In 1980, the Ansals had bought a plot for a cinema hall in Saket. Anupam opened in 1983. A decade later, the theatre was leased out to the PVR group on the condition that it would be converted into Delhi's first multiplex. Thus the Ansals and Ajay Bijli, the man behind the PVR leisure world, introduced the concept of multiplexes to India's capital in 1995. In 2004, the Anupam property was sold to the Bijlis.

This was Sushil's second movie theatre investment. In 1972 he had bought a 2,480-square-yard plot in Green Park from R.C. Sood and Company (now the Eros Group) and the Uphaar cinema was commissioned a year later. This was hardly a big part of the Ansal business, but it was to play a tragic role in Sushil's life. The Uphaar chapter must, however, wait for later.

As two decades of manic growth in Delhi began to wind down, Sushils' reputation as one of India's biggest real-estate tycoons had been burnished. He was a name to be reckoned with in Delhi's

■ MARRIOT WELCOME HOTEL
In Delhi's Saket area, it was built as a joint venture with ITC Hotels, 1993 – 1995

business circles, where the overhaul of the Connaught Place region was indelibly linked to the Ansals. So was the development of district centres of Nehru Place, Bhikaji Cama Place, Rajender Place, Saket and Laxmi Nagar.

The real gainer in this period, however, was a rapacious, extortionate entity called the DDA. "It simply minted money," as an old Ansal associate puts it, "and was at one time considered the world's largest landowner." As a consequence of the 1961 Master Plan, the DDA acquired 55,000 acres of land in Delhi, primarily from farmers. The private sector was banned from buying agricultural land for residential

Left to right

THOSE WERE THE DAYS
Sushil and Kusum with Italian movie star Gina Lollobrigida at a film festival in Uphaar

INDIA'S MOVIE QUEEN
Felicitating Rekha at a film event in Uphaar

THE ENTERTAINER
Welcoming Raj Kapoor at a movie premiere in Uphaar

purposes; this was a DDA monopoly. As the sole buyer, DDA bought cheap, often at no more than Rs 10,000 an acre. However, it released land in dribs and drabs, pushed up the market by limiting supply, encouraged wild bidding at auctions and sold at prices that resembled Rs 10 crore an acre and more. It claimed it was doing so in the interests of providing housing to the poor, in which it, unfortunately, has a dismal record.

In some manner, this was exploitation by the government in the name of cross-subsidising budget housing. In actual practice, the DDA, as emphasised by the Public Accounts Committee of Parliament, has grossly mismanaged its funds, is highly inefficient and defeated the very objective for which it was set up: to provide sufficient housing and commercial space in Delhi and keep property prices and rentals in check. Due to the DDA's monopoly and its failure to deliver, Delhi's residents have suffered. In the words of a former Prime Minister, the

DDA's housing schemes have only succeeded in giving its customers "pigeon holes" to live in.

In his heart, Sushil knew that this was not right. He was also unhappy that areas like Nehru Place had been so shabbily planned and designed by the DDA and other agencies which did not, for instance, outsource creative activity to any capable private service providers, as is done across the world. By the 1980s, Sushil had begun to long for a real-estate industry free of DDA-type shackles and started to lobby the government to loosen the chains. It would be a long and determined fight.

Left to right

ALONGSIDE GLAMOUR
Sushil and Kusum with Indrani Rehman, the first Miss India

BEHIND THE CAMERA
Sushil at a film shoot with friends Saeed Jaffrey and Anand Mahindroo

PHASE THREE

EXPANDING THE LANDSCAPE

Mention the year 1991 to Indian tycoons of a certain generation – roughly, anybody above sixty – and you are bound to get an immediate and instinctive response. The eyes usually say it. In some cases, they light up: 1991 was the year of liberalisation, the starting point of economic deregulation and reform and of the perception that India might just be a twenty-first-century miracle. Other eyes turn dull and sad. To an old guard that flourished under the licence-permit raj, 1991 signals the end of an era.

If you ask Sushil Ansal about the impact of 1991, he is relatively non-committal, almost searching for an answer. In truth, the budget and new industrial policy of 1991 saw dramatic changes for the financial services, manufacturing and trade. They did precious little for the housing or real estate sector. Genuine reform in Sushil's area of business was still a long way and, in fact, has not effectively happened even in the first decade of the new millennium. That aside, 1991 sparked no dramatic new venture, marked no inflection point. Rather, it caught Sushil bang in the middle of a ten-year-long run of expansion and diversification into new geographies, both in the country and abroad.

By the early 1980s, Sushil had come to realise there was a limit to what he could achieve in Delhi. "There was a sense of frustration," he explains, "that a monopoly in the form of the DDA was not allowing our creative energies to be used to their potential." He began to look just south of Delhi, to Haryana and Gurgaon. It was in 1980 that the Ansals conceived Palam Vihar, the second planned, privately-built township in Gurgaon closely following DLF. On November 19, 1985, Sushil's company got a licence from the Haryana government to develop 109 acres, the first phase of Palam Vihar, a township now spread across 650 acres.

Preceding page, top left
ANOTHER MILESTONE
An Ansal residential complex in Gurgaon

Preceding page, bottom left
DIVERSIFICATION
N.D. Tiwari, former chief minister of Uttar Pradesh, at the earth-breaking ceremony of the Ansal Paper Mill in Sikandrabad

Preceding page, bottom right
DELHI'S FIRST MALL
The iconic amphitheatre of Ansal Plaza

Preceding page, top right
SUSHANT LOK
The Ansal mini-city in Gurgaon

Facing page
CELEBRITY HOMES, GURGAON
A popular Ansal project for NRIs

Unlike Delhi, Haryana had enacted a business-friendly and enlightened township development law. The regulatory authorities allowed developers to use 55 per cent of their land for plotted development and the rest for social infrastructure – roads, parks, community centres, schools, hospitals and so on. The experiment called Gurgaon began cautiously. "We started buying land in 1982," says Sushil, "at one lakh rupees an acre. Today, it is four to five crore rupees an acre in Palam Vihar. In Sushant Lok, it is seven to eight crore rupees an acre." For the customer, the price rise has been even sharper.

The Palam Vihar story began by selling plots at Rs 250 per square yard (today's market price is about Rs. 40,000 a square yard while at Sushant Lok, which started a year later, the prices are around Rs. 80,000 to Rs. 1 lakh per square yard). Families that were priced out of the South Delhi market and speculative investors were the first to put down their money. DLF had already floated its township 1.5 years before Sushil entered the market. In order to avoid direct competition, Sushil thought of selling built-up homes and cottages instead of just plots which DLF was doing. On one of his visits to Bangkok, he inspected some designs for villas and engaged a firm of Thai architects to design French and continental villas for Palam Vihar. Construction was Sushil's forte and he soon erected furnished sample villas for customers to see. Buyers who wanted to avoid the headache of building a house welcomed the idea of a ready-made villa.

Creating a township in the middle of nowhere was very different from selling office space in the middle of bustling Connaught Place. Sushil and his colleagues had to conjure up a whole neighbourhood and sense of community. "We opened our school, Chiranjeev Bharti, which was started by Kusum. By 1986 end, people were moving in. Today, of course, Palam Vihar has multiplexes, the Ansal Plaza mall, several schools and hospitals such as the Columbia Asia Hospital."

It was another universe twenty years ago. Palam Vihar and Sushant Lok took their time to become both inhabited and inhabitable, but Sushil never lost faith. "Build and they will come" was his unspoken motto. In a sense K.P. Singh and he pioneered the private townships of Gurgaon, inventing the wheel that others were to use. "As roads were aligned, we planted trees to make the colony attractive," he says, "Palam Vihar has half a million trees. We provided social

17

infrastructure as quickly as we could, even arranging for transport." The Ansals ran buses to and from Palam Vihar and four points in Delhi, to facilitate those who had moved to the township.

East of National Highway 8, in another part of Gurgaon, Sushil got a licence to develop 101 acres. Today, this project has expanded to 750 acres and is called Sushant Lok I, in the heart of New Gurgaon. A distress sale by another developer, Utility Builders and Leasing Ltd., had the Ansals getting a further 184 acres in July 1991.This became the core of Sushant Lok II. It was a tough deal because Utility Builders' township license had been cancelled due to breach of conditions. Customers were thronging for a refund. Sushil bailed out the company by buying its shares, getting the license breach rectified, having the license reinstated and promising Utility Builder's customers that he would honour prior commitments to them. A separate area was bought from another company, Aadarshila Developers in January 1996 and earmarked for Sushank Lok III.

In 2010, Sushil returned to Gurgaon with a high-end project called Escencia. Initially being built over 111 acres, though more land is

ANSALS HI-RISE CITY
Sushil helped make Gurgaon the shining metropolis it is today

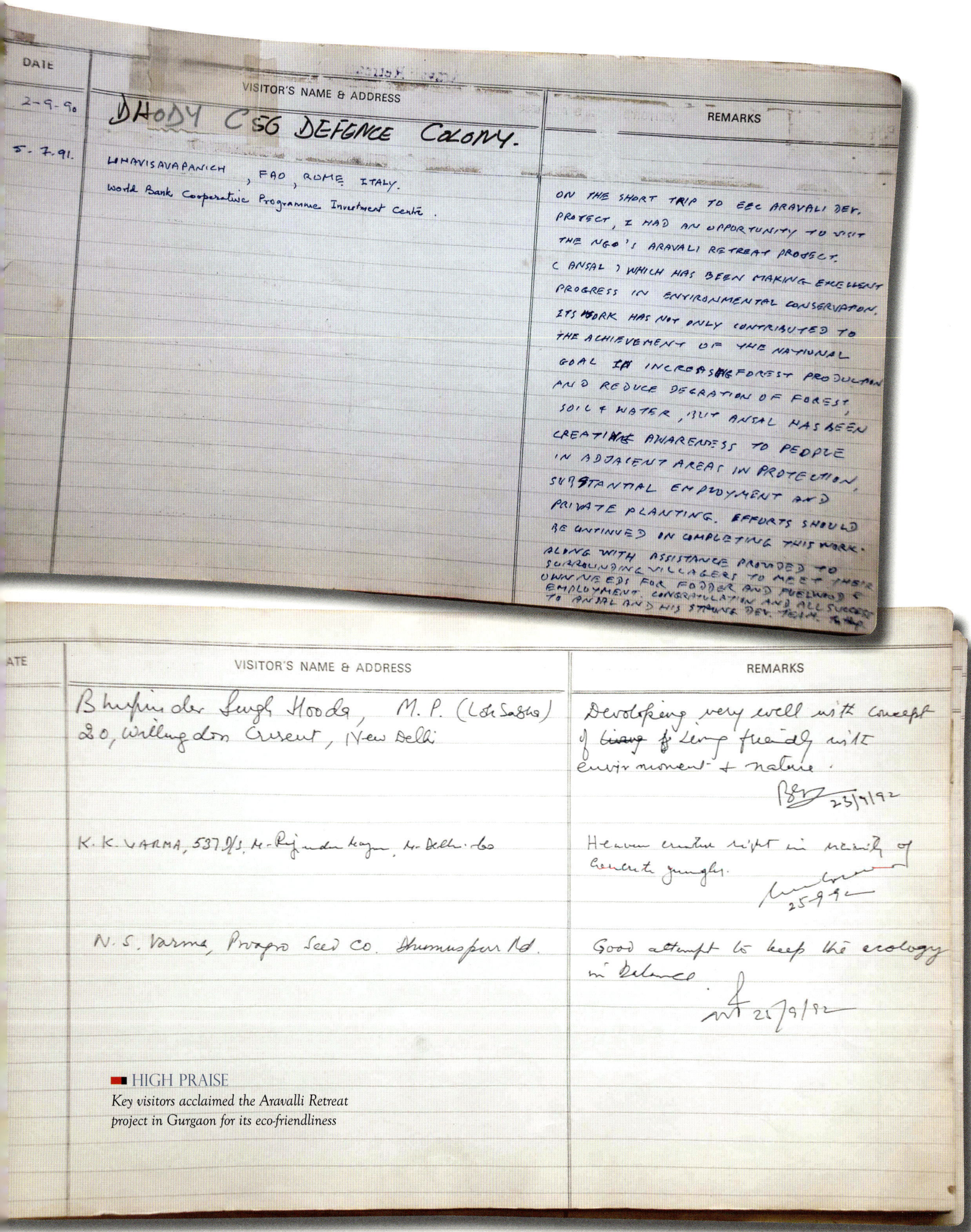

DATE	VISITOR'S NAME & ADDRESS	REMARKS
2-9-90	DHODY C 56 DEFENCE COLONY.	
5-7-91	L. HAVISAVAPANICH, FAO, ROME ITALY. World Bank Cooperative Programme Investment Centre.	ON THE SHORT TRIP TO EEC ARAVALI DEV. PROJECT, I HAD AN OPPORTUNITY TO VISIT THE NGO'S ARAVALI RETREAT PROJECT (ANSAL) WHICH HAS BEEN MAKING EXCELLENT PROGRESS IN ENVIRONMENTAL CONSERVATION. ITS WORK HAS NOT ONLY CONTRIBUTED TO THE ACHIEVEMENT OF THE NATIONAL GOAL IN INCREASING FOREST PRODUCTION AND REDUCE DEGRATION OF FOREST, SOIL & WATER, BUT ANSAL HAS BEEN CREATING AWARENESS TO PEOPLE IN ADJACENT AREAS IN PROTECTION, SUBSTANTIAL EMPLOYMENT AND PRIVATE PLANTING. EFFORTS SHOULD BE CONTINUED IN COMPLETING THIS WORK ALONG WITH ASSISTANCE PROVIDED TO SURROUNDING VILLAGERS TO MEET THEIR OWN NEEDS FOR FODDER AND FUELWOOD & EMPLOYMENT. CONGRATULATION AND ALL SUCCESS TO ANSAL AND HIS STRONG DEV. TEAM.

DATE	VISITOR'S NAME & ADDRESS	REMARKS
	Bhupinder Singh Hooda, M.P. (Lok Sabha) 20, Willingdon Crescent, New Delhi	Developing very well with concept of living friendly with environment + nature. [illegible] 23/9/92
	K.K. VARMA, 537 D/S, N-Rajinder Nagar, N. Delhi-60	Heaven on earth right in vicinity of concrete jungles. [illegible] 25-9-92
	N.S. Varma, Pro Agro Seed Co. [illegible] Rd.	Good attempt to keep the ecology in balance. [illegible] 25/9/92

HIGH PRAISE

Key visitors acclaimed the Aravalli Retreat project in Gurgaon for its eco-friendliness

being bought and it will grow to 200 acres, this will be the first 'all green', eco-friendly township in Gurgaon.

The obsession with green development is not new for Sushil. One of his favourite projects involved regenerating the Aravalli Hills that stretch across Haryana and extend into Delhi. This took the form of the Aravalli Retreat, developed in the period between 1989 and 1991. A nature lover from his college days – he went trekking in the Himalayas in 1958 and 1959 – Sushil was struck by the damage being done to the Aravallis. One day, while driving though Sohna, just outside Gurgaon, he noticed how reckless cutting of trees and busy stone quarries had ravaged the hills. Sushil decided he had to do something, and sought to give back to society by launching a hill regeneration programme as a pilot project. He put together 1,200 acres of uncultivable terrain in the Raisina Hills, part of the Aravallis, He engaged R.S. Randhawa, a well known landscapist and horticulturist. After getting approval from the Haryana Government, he went ahead and planted over 100,000 trees, created dams and dykes for harvesting rain water, and also stopped soil erosion from hilly slopes. Soil was dumped in several patches to increase the soil cover. Land use was changed to preserve the site as a farm area. Man-made lakes were developed, as ducks and other birds migrated to the location. This project is at an elevation of 500 to 750 feet. Today, it is the greenest area in the Aravalli range. Interestingly, when the project was in the development stage, a group of environmentalists brought a stay order from the Supreme Court. Any meddling with nature by human beings leads to degradation of the environment and not upgrade was their plea. However, after several months in court, Sushil's lawyers convinced the judges of their good intentions and the Supreme Court blessed the project. Today, the bird population in the area has increased manifold and Aravalli Retreat is a haven for bird watchers, with even Siberian cranes spotted in the right season. The air is also clearer and less polluted. The moon and stars seem to be touchable at night.

On July 5, 1991, Aravalli Retreat was visited by a World Bank team that included environmental experts. Having experienced the atmosphere, the team wrote in the visitors' book "(We) had an opportunity to visit the NGO's Aravalli Retreat project (Ansal), which

(We) had an opportunity to visit the NGO's Aravalli Retreat project (Ansal), which has been making excellent progress in environmental conservation. Its work has not only contributed to the achievement of the national goal in increasing forest production and reduce degradation of forest, soil and water, but Ansal has been creating awareness to people in adjacent areas in protection, substantial employment and private planting. Efforts should be continued on completing this work. Along with assistance provided to surrounding villagers to meet their own needs for fodder and fuel wood and employment. Congratulation and all success to Ansal and his strong development team".

Comments by the World Bank team which visited the project in 1991.

has been making excellent progress in environmental conservation. Its work has not only contributed to the achievement of the national goal in increasing forest production and reduce degradation of forest, soil and water, but Ansal has been creating awareness to people in adjacent areas in protection, substantial employment and private planting. Efforts should be continued on completing this work. Along with assistance provided to surrounding villagers to meet their own needs for fodder and fuel wood and employment. Congratulation and all success to Ansal and his strong development team."

A little later, Bhupinder Singh Hooda, currently Chief Minister of Haryana but then a Member of the Lok Sabha, visited Aravalli Retreat. He made a pithy remark in the visitors book: "Developing very well with concept of being friendly with environment and nature." Sushil modestly disclaims: "This environment upgradation was possible because Vinod Kumar Saigal, an eminent engineer heading the construction wing, got

REFUGE FROM THE CROWD
Sushil's farmhouse in Bijwasan, on the outskirts of Delhi

SHEETAL KUNJ, ARAVALI RETREAT
Sushil's first green project, before the concept became a trend

passionately involved, working day and night to make this a success. He is very emotionally involved in this exemplary and different project."

Incidentally, Sushil also created two other farmhouse collectives for Delhi's citizens. Ansals Farm Villas in Satbari, near the Chhattarpur Temple, has over 100 farmhouses on two-acre plots. The other project is in Pushpanjali, near the Indira Gandhi Airport. It has 150 farmhouses, one of which is Sushil's very own escape from the maddening crowd of Delhi.

If Gurgaon represented one aspect of Sushil's attempt to look beyond Delhi, overseas projects were another. The Ansal brand travelled to several countries: Iraq, Russia, Thailand, Vietnam, Nepal and Bangladesh. The company played both developer and contractor. Sushil is frank that the initial motivation to seeking projects abroad was the prospect of tax breaks. "Fifty per cent of income in foreign exchange was tax free," he says, "and this was a big incentive." He also welcomed the chance of better exposure to international contracting and real estate methodologies and practices.

The first port of call was Iraq. In the early 1970s, Saddam Hussein was still seen as a progressive, benevolent dictator rather than the megalomaniac warmonger he became by the 1990s, and Iraq was transforming itself through an oil-fuelled construction boom. In fact, when Sushil first visited Iraq in 1976, scouting for opportunities, he found the Iraqi strongman "using oil money productively, building steel and cement plants and promoting adult education." This was unlike many other oil economies in the Gulf region, which wasted their money in creating showy symbols that were not long-term assets.

The first contract from Baghdad came in 1979. The Ansals were asked to build factory sheds in a coded project named Saad 3. These were no ordinary factory sheds, but encompassed half a million square feet just outside Baghdad. Intricate cable channels and complicated machine foundations were part of the blueprint. Yet, the contractors weren't told everything. "We did not know what machines would be installed there," recalls Sushil, "and only vaguely guessed it was a military installation." It later emerged Saad 3 was put to use during the Iran war and the First Gulf War as a weapon factory.

The next project saw Sushil go to Mosul in the north of Iraq and execute the construction of grain silos and godowns, a project not

very different from the one he had begun with all those years ago in Hapur. "Conditions were harsh here," says Sushil, "and also unique. The area was underdeveloped. We carried water, cement and bricks on donkey-back." The jewel in the crown was Tahrir Square, a modern office building in Baghdad that, when completed in 1990, was the tallest office building in the Iraqi capital. Years later, Sushil was to read about Tahrir Square in newspapers. It was targeted by the US Air Force in the Second Gulf War and, being a central location in the Iraqi capital, subsequently became a favourite spot for suicide bombings by Islamist insurgents. One missile did hit the building and damaged it.

Iraq was a massive learning experience. By the early 1980s, Baghdad and other big cities were attracting leading construction companies. Sushil could benchmark his work against American and European counterparts and against Chinese companies that paid their workers in kind, the workers' families being paid cash back home in

OVERSEAS FORAY, 1980
The Tahir Square complex in Baghdad

China. Sushil too took 1,500 workers from his home country, feeding and housing them. The workers were paid in dollars in Baghdad and then repatriated the money to their families in India. In a time of chronic foreign exchange shortage, the Ansals and other developers such as J.P. & Associates, Somdatts, Bhandari Builders, Continental Constructions, Unitech and so on were doing a great service to India. The Ansal group won awards for two successive years for highest repatriation of foreign exchange in the construction services sector.

In 1990, Sushil took his team to Thailand, seeing scope for real-estate development and not merely contracting. The Thai voyage was the culmination of policy change in India. For years, the Indian government had allowed Indian contracting companies to go abroad (and execute projects that would earn foreign exchange) but not real-estate developers to do so (since they would need to initially spend foreign exchange in making capital investments and buying land and material). It was a

THAI PROJECTS WITH PARTNER KIRIT SHAH
Prestige Towers, Bangkok

ALSO IN BANGKOK
Palm Court Service Apartments

regressive policy that did not allow business to grow. Sushil had protested against it vigorously and, finally, it was amended.

In Thailand, the Ansals partnered with an Indian expatriate named Kirit Shah, who was introduced to Sushil by a common friend, Deepak Mittal, a senior executive with the Aditya Birla Group in Thailand, in a joint venture called Maxwin Ansal Ltd. It bought its first plot of land in Bangkok in 1989. The partners built six multi-storeyed apartment blocks in Bangkok, and were the contractors for the four-star Hotel Atrium. Kirit Shah also introduced Sushil to another Thai developer, Mr. Prosong, and they executed a few projects together. Vinod Kumar Saigal, Sushil's brother-in-law, drove this initiative in Thailand and ensured that the Ansals and their partners delivered high-quality construction within the specified time. The success of the Thai projects encouraged Shah and Sushil to look at other neighbouring countries and secured a project in Vietnam to be built in collaboration with the Vietnamese Military Housing Board. While the West View Residency complex was being built, however, Maxwin Ansal sold the project to another company and left Hanoi. The Asian flu of 1997 and the devaluation of the Thai baht led to an exit from South-east Asia. The Ansals were also having second thoughts as the Thai authorities were not allowing Indian labour, robbing Sushil of a key comparative advantage.

Above
GOING ABROAD
The Baan Suan Lalanah complex was another of Sushil's Thai projects

Below
NEW FRONTIERS
Sushil and Vinod Saigal (extreme right) with their business partner in Vietnam, Kirit Shah (extreme Left)

In 1997, the Ansals also ended work on two hotels in Russia – in Novgorod and Pskov. The breakup of the Soviet Union and the post-perestroika opportunities in Russia had created space for Sushil and he had travelled to Moscow in 1993. The labour used was Indian and almost 500 workers were taken for these projects. Towards the end, the rouble began to depreciate and the client went bankrupt. Two successive bills were dishonoured. With 90 per cent of the work done, the Ansals packed up and came home. The Russian projects also marked the initiation of Pranav, Sushil's son into the world of contracting. He assisted his uncle Gopal. Pranav and his wife Sheetal spent a little over a year in Russia while work was on. It was a great learning experience for them.

There were other foreign projects: an expressway in Bangladesh; a 300-apartment budget housing complex in Kathmandu. Yet, by the mid-1990s, Sushil decided it was time to focus on India with renewed vigour. The India story was beginning to gear up.

India's renewal had begun, of course, in the summer of 1991. The story is well known. There was political uncertainty in the first half of that year, an early election

Above left
TO FOREIGN SHORES
At a business dinner during the building of the hotel in Pskov, Russia

Above right
RUSSIA TRYST
With clients during the construction of the hotel in Novgorod

Below
LIVING THE MOMENT
Holidaying in the snows of Moscow

THE INNER COUNCIL
Pranav stands next to his father in the Ansal API boardroom

had been called and a combination of governmental and economic instability had wrecked national morale. Foreign exchange reserves had dropped precipitously, a balance of payments crisis gripped the country and international financial institutions more or less gave up on India. So low was India's credit rating that the government had to mortgage a portion of its gold reserves. India was on the edge of insolvency.

This situation was not entirely unexpected. It had a context, and had been building up for about two years. The property sector is extremely income and optimism sensitive and Sushil was beginning to read the bad news a little earlier than many others. "Sentiment was down in India since about 1988-89," he remembers, "we experienced the impact in the real estate market. The momentum of price and rental increases began to slow down. The trend was still upward but the curve had flattened. Real estate companies had stopped growing." To some extent, Sushil's projects in Iraq insulated him from the worst but it was still a worrying scenario.

The reformist policies announced by the P.V. Narasimha Rao government were not of direct relevance to real estate developers but did provide collateral benefit. Financial services deregulation freed up capital. Banks were allowed to lend a larger part of their surplus to the housing sector and to developers. "This was to be used as bridging finance," Sushil explains, "for completion of housing projects." Attempts were also made to liberalise lending to end-use purchasers and by the mid-1990s were beginning to create a new class of home owners. "Earlier even small loans were available only to wealthy individuals," says Sushil, "and at exorbitant 12 to 15 per cent interest rates for home buyers. Now more people came into a position to buy homes. People began to move from rental housing to ownership."

The first flush of reforms also unleashed unreal expectations about the size and trajectory of the Indian economy and domestic consumption. MNCs came rushing in and paid a premium for office space. Commercial rentals in Connaught Place, in the buildings Sushil and the Ansals had built, hit unbelievable heights. The idea of Gurgaon as not just a residential suburb but as an alternative business city, especially for the new service sector companies, began to take root. Ansals joined the endeavours of DLF, which came to property development after three decades and more or less re-imagined Gurgaon. Later, newer players such as Unitech came in as well.

In the short run, there was speculation and a property bubble was created by 1994. Yet, it was impossible to ignore that the contours of the market were changing. "A new type of longer-term, stable buyer had emerged," goes Sushil's assessment. "It wanted quality housing and it also wanted modern office buildings. We had to build for a more contemporary India. We were catering to committed buyers, not quick-buck speculators."

However, it was not all rosy. Sushil sensed that real estate developers were becoming over-invested in Delhi and the National Capital Region and was cautious enough to want to avoid this. He was keen to move to other states and, on the model of Haryana, build townships. The impetus for this reform would have to come from state governments, as real estate was a state subject under the Constitution of India. In most major states, developers were only allowed to venture into small group housing schemes and in Delhi, as already explained, even that was constricted. Builders were not permitted to develop large areas of land as the DDA would not loosen its monopoly.

The 1991 reforms didn't really do much for real-estate developers. There was recognition that laws such as the Urban Land Ceiling (ULCRA) were negative and created an artificial scarcity. "Its repercussions were strong," Sushil says, "it froze supply and hampered housing creation in our biggest cities." Even so, removing ULCRA (some critics prefer the acronym ULCER) was not an easy, one-stage process. It required the concurrence of state governments, and states such as Maharashtra only gave permission for repeal in 2007.

At the federal level, real-estate developers felt they were discriminated against by the Finance Ministry. "India treats dollars differently," exclaims Sushil. "A hotelier who earns foreign exchange from a tourist gets tax exemption as does a rice exporter who sells rice abroad. A real-estate developer who sells a flat to an NRI customer gets no tax break. I once brought this up with a senior bureaucrat in the Finance Ministry at a pre-Budget meeting. I was told that by selling to NRIs developers were actually adding to the housing shortage in the country."

It became Sushil's business to lobby and build public opinion against such regressive and repressive laws and regulations. He was not alone. The big guns of real estate fired together, competitors worked

THE TRINITY

Seen here on the cover of a magazine, Sushil, DLF's K.P. Singh (left) and Unitech's Ramesh Chandra are the titans of real-estate development in India –and good friends

as comrades for their collective weal. K.P. Singh, the patriarch and chairman of DLF and a fellow doyen of the industry, recalls those days with excitement: "We worked as colleagues and not rivals on several policy issues – doggedly lobbying for change. There were vast areas of common interest even within a competitive framework. Sushil and I, along with Ramesh Chandra of Unitech, were part of the same struggle against the government."

Sushil was among the earliest to see the potential of smaller cities – the so-called Tier I and Tier II towns – and the "hunger for well-planned housing" with good amenities and interiors. Even while waiting for the rules to change and allow him to build whole townships, he took Ansal API, as the flagship company was now known, to a variety of second-tier cities. (API was originally Ansal Properties and Industries Ltd. In 2004, it was renamed Ansal Properties and Infrastructure). By 2005 Ansal API was busy at construction sites in fifteen cities over five states.

As early as 1993, the Ansals had a pan-Indian presence. "We also went to Bangalore (1992) and Cochin (1995)" Says Sushil, "and to Agra (1985), Allahabad (1989) and Ghaziabad." In 1993, Sushil had entered the Mumbai market with a group housing project in Borivali East.

The most ambitious undertaking of the time was in Lucknow. The Ashiana sub-city – 400 acres on the Kanpur Road, very close to the airport in Amausi that Sushil's father had helped construct in the aftermath of the war of 1962 – was being developed by the Lucknow Development Authority (LDA). "Somehow the LDA kept running into problems," says Sushil, "and eventually they sold the undeveloped land to us. Ashiana came up in the early 1990s, symbolising our expansion period."

The experience of developing Palam Vihar and Sushant Lok made it clear to Sushil that genuine township development, with its mix of residential and commercial space, social and leisure infrastructure, was not only profitable, it was also professionally satisfying. It provided a model that finally unchained the developer from tardy municipal and civic agencies that might or might not deliver on their obligations.

The all-important step was to convince other state governments to replicate Haryana's urban incubation law and build genuine partnerships with private developers. Sushil travelled relentlessly and spoke to literally dozens of chief ministers. "By the end 1990s," Sushil reports, "we were beginning to find an audience. After the Haryana success story, other states had seen the potential. Directly or indirectly, the housing sector affects 250 industries, from cement to electrical fittings to textiles. As such it is a huge employer. After agriculture, it is the second largest employer." No politician could run away from such compelling logic.

Even then, results were slow to come. The Ansals went to Rajasthan in 1995 and urged the government to change policy. "We told them of the Haryana model," Sushil says, "and how it had the smallest percentage of unauthorised colonies." It took eight years to convince the government to change its policies. It was only in 2003 that the agreement to develop Sushant City in Jaipur was signed. Today, it has a 400-acre spread. Pranav Ansal was assigned the responsibility for growth and expansion in Rajasthan.

This encouraged Pranav and Sushil to spread to other small cities like Jodhpur, Ajmer, Bhilwara and Bikaner. In Jodhpur, they signed an agreement with Gaj Singh, the former Maharaja and developed the first shopping-cum-multiplex complex. Another heritage property of Maharaja Gaj Singh is Rai Ka Bagh Palace. Sushil and his son-in-law, Vipin Luthra, are partnering with Gaj Singh in developing a heritage hotel. Today Ansal API is the largest private developer in Rajasthan.

While professionalizing his company and giving it an all-India identity, Sushil planned to go public in the November 1992. The first public issue, for Ansal Properties, was successful and was oversubscribed by six times. After three years, Sushil and his brothers decided to take two other companies, Ansal Buildwell and Ansal Housing, public. Funds were arranged from the capital market by the three Ansal companies at a time when the real-estate sector was not the darling of the stock market. (Having three different companies turned out to be a blessing when the family partition took place in 1998 and the three brothers went their own ways. The mother company Ansal Properties, now Ansal API, came to the share of Sushil).

Emotionally Sushil was keen to do business in his home state. As early as 2000, Pranav had started projects in Punjab by building shopping malls in Ludhiana and Jalandhar. The success of these two cities took Pranav to Mohali and Amritsar. The Ansals are now developing a 300-acre Golf Links township in Mohali, adjoining Chandigarh and an integrated commercial cum housing project is under implementation in Amritsar.

"We worked as colleagues and not rivals on several policy issues – doggedly lobbying for change. There were vast areas of common interest even within a competitive framework. Sushil and I, along with Ramesh Chandra of Unitech, were part of the same struggle against the government."

K.P. Singh
Chairman of DLF

In Haryana, Gurgaon was getting over-crowded. In December 2003, Ansal API got a license to develop Sushant City in Kundli (Sonepat), just four kilometres from Delhi. Today, this is a 250-acre township, right off National Highway 1. Sushil was the first major developer to move into Sonepat, also in Haryana but to the north of Delhi. His company began building and promoting residential townships in Panipat, Kurukshetra, Karnal and Yamunanagar, expanding its catchment area in Haryana to well beyond Gurgaon and giving Delhi a whole range of ancillary cities. With the imminent arrival of the Delhi Metro and the widening of National Highway 1, he is convinced that the next growth area is the Kundli-Sonepat-Panipat belt.

Actually, 2003 was a breakthrough year as it was also when Uttar Pradesh announced its policy of "Hi-Tech Cities" and essentially incorporated many of the suggestions that township developers such as the Ansals had been pushing. The Uttar Pradesh projects, particularly in the Greater Noida-Bulandshahr region 40 minutes east of Delhi, are expected to define API's evolution in the coming decades, till about 2025 (*see chapter* 7).

Whether in Rajasthan or Uttar Pradesh or Punjab, the townships that were conceived in 2003 and the policies and legislations that underpinned them were actually the fruit of Sushil's labour a decade earlier, in the mid-1990s. He had been the catalyst for policy change. Years after the liberalisation of 1991, pragmatism and a fair and equitable opportunity for private sector developers were beginning to be accepted in state after state. For Sushil and his generation of real estate entrepreneurs, this was a long-awaited triumph.

Only in one city did Sushil continue to have his hopes and aspirations for a better regulatory matrix thwarted and crushed: Delhi, his own home town. In his capacity as Chairman of the National Housing Committee of the Federation of Indian Chambers of Commerce and Industry (FICCI) and as President of both the PHDCCI and the Rajdhani Promoters and Builders Association, Sushil requested and pleaded with the DDA and with the Union Ministry of Urban Development to relax the DDA's monopoly and give private developers a chance to mitigate the housing shortage in the city, and enhance standards.

As PHDCCI President, he even presented a specific proposal that promised, provided private developers were allowed to aggregate land, that flats would be built and sold at rates lower than those the DDA was charging its EWS (economically weaker sections) and LIG (low income group) customers. If accepted, this could have gone some way in solving Delhi's pressing housing problem. The DDA and the Ministry just turned up their noses. "Committees were set up but nothing really happened," rues Sushil, "refined contracting was allowed, not quite private development. This remains a matter of regret... that I couldn't do more for mass housing in a city I so love and cherish."

However, as an industry leader, Sushil was widely respected and had an enviable profile. Between 1989 and 1991, he served as the Chairman of the Overseas Construction Council of India. After Kuwait had been liberated by American-led forces in March 1991, Sushil had led a delegation to United States. The idea was to win contracting and sub-contracting business from American construction lines that were going to rebuild Kuwait. As President of the PHDCCI in 2001-02, he led government industry delegations to China, Hong Kong and

Above left
VOICE OF BUSINESS
Speaking at a FICCI function as Chairman of the National Housing Commission

Above right
A CITIZEN OF DELHI
At a public function with Chief Minister Shiela Dixit

BUILDING LIFESTYLES

AERODROME, AMRITSAR

GOLF LINKS, MOHALI

CITY CENTRE, MOHALI

IT SEZ, GREATER NOIDA

IVY, GURGAON

EXPAND TERRITORY

Ansal API projects in various cities across northern India

TULIP SUSHANT CITY, JAIPUR

SUSHANT CITY, ICON VILLA, AJMER

SUSHANT CITY, BHILWARA

SUSHANT CITY, BIKANER

SUNSHINE COUNTY, KUNDLI

Korea and was among the first to recommend that Indian regulatory systems learn from the Chinese Special Economic Zone (SEZ) model. In November 2003, as Chairman of the India-Canada Joint Business Council and India-Canada Bilateral Committee, Sushil led a trade, technology and investment delegation to Ottawa, Toronto, Vancouver and Montreal.

In the midst of all this, Sushil also gave Delhi its first modern shopping mall: Ansal Plaza on Khel Gaon Marg, which opened on November 14, 1999. For a whole host of reasons, it was one of the toughest assignments of his career. "Bidding for the plot opened in 1993," says Sushil, "at a time when the markets were at their peak. We bid unrealistically. The reserve price for the project, which had a proposed 170,000 square feet of built up area, was Rs. 45 crore. We came up with Rs. 157 crores. Unitech was the second highest with Rs. 103 crores."

Even so, despite the challenging numbers, it still seemed an attractive proposition. The Ansals started selling shops on the ground floor for Rs. 20,000 a square foot. That was double the purchase price. "If you added Rs. 3,000 per square foot for construction, we were still expecting Rs. 7,000 per square foot, or a total of Rs. 114 crore, as profit." Soon enough, 30 per cent of the shopping mall had been sold to various investors and retailers.

Then came the crash of 1996. "To be fair I saw it coming," Sushil admits, "but couldn't predict the timing." It was clear to Sushil that the crazy price rise in the Delhi property market was just not sustainable. The Ansals were not hit badly because Sushil had been cautious. He had not hoarded stock but persisted with the volumes game and sold – in some cases at peak prices – as soon as he finished a building. He had also taken the group to smaller towns, where the quantum of the decline was not as sharp as it had been in Delhi. However, there was one pitfall even Sushil found hard to negotiate: Ansal Plaza.

It wasn't just the market crash. A range of crises happened together. The Uphaar tragedy (*see chapter* 4) and the family partition that saw the Ansal group split three ways also had a significant impact on Ansal Plaza. "When the family restructuring took place," Sushil explains, "Ansal Plaza came as part of my share." He refused to believe it was a dud and that he would not deliver on his promises.

Notwithstanding all his problems, Sushil fought back: "We reduced prices from Rs 20-21,000 a square foot to Rs 13-14,000 a square foot, even compensating those who had bought at higher prices. Our profits dipped very sharply but we saved goodwill." Strapped for cash, it was sometimes difficult to pay suppliers and contractors. "We offered them barter deals," confides Sushil, "giving plots in Sushant Lok and Palam Vihar in lieu of cash."

Nevertheless, when Ansal Plaza opened in the winter of 1999, 60,000 square feet – over a third of the built-up area – remained unsold. Today, the Ansals retain and earn rent from 35,000 square feet. The rest has been sold; the market price is Rs 30,000 a square foot. More important, Ansal Plaza heralded a revolution in Delhi's retail and shopping culture. Today Ansal API has eight malls in operations in different cities in India. Four more malls are being built or planned.

Ansal Plaza represented a wrenching struggle that ended on a happy note. However, one memory of that period lingers and continues to haunt. The events of Friday, June 13, 1997 – the real-life "Friday the 13th" that so scarred Sushil's life – had widespread implications. The horrific Uphaar fire and its aftermath merit a separate chapter.

A MAGAZINE INTERVIEW

The headline says it all

SPONSORED FEATURE

Anjolie Ela Menon, Satish Gujral and MF Husain decorate Vishranti's walls

The brick and mortar man

He was once blamed for 'altering Delhi's skyline.' But after four decades in the construction business, today he is heralded as a pioneer in the field. As SUSHIL ANSAL'S company, Ansal Properties and Infrastructure, luxuriously spreads to small towns and cities, this gentleman is happy. Over a relaxed lunch at his palatial house *Vishranti*, he tells JAYITA BANDYOPADHYAY about how he got his surname, his *avant garde* business ideas, his love for golf and *ghar ka khana*

Ansal is a rare surname...
My father's name was Lala Chiranjiv Lal. Somehow, I never liked the surname. So when I got admitted to school, my mother offered to change my surname to Asal, meaning pure. But in school, Asal became a butt of jokes. So one day I inserted the 'n', just like that. And Ansal it has been from then on. It's an original creation.

Like your business. But wasn't it your father who started it?
We hail from Punjab's Hoshiarpur district where my father was a Railway employee. He moved to Delhi as a school teacher. Later he quit that to become a sub-contractor. I joined him in the 60s and set up the company in '67.

Your father wanted you to be in the IAS.
While I was at St Stephen's (graduated in 60), I studied hard but had no inclination to join services. So I didn't take the UPSC exam, opting for a correspondence course in business administration instead.

When you joined the business with the then tallest building in the city, Akashdeep, many were angry.
Delhi's Master Plan was just out in 1969 when we planned Akashdeep. We took advantage of the new Plan and constructed the highrise at Barakhamba Road. It was a landmark. People blamed me for altering Delhi's skyline. But I knew then that the city had to reach out to the skies. We followed up with business centres at Nehru Place and Bhikaji Cama Place.

The mural on the outer façade of Akashdeep was also a first of its kind...
It was done by a deaf and dumb artist. He had been sitting idle and wante[d] him a chance. He did every[thing] ... burnt the tiles himself. Tha[t] ... colours have not faded. ... Shankar's Doll Museum ... Indian Standards Buildin[g] ... Bahadur Shah Zafar M[arg] ... trend of murals on pub[lic] ... preserve art. In Italy, th[e] ... art and architecture in ... The public can enjoy ... well as keep them saf[e] ... and we don't preser[ve] ...

When you intro[duced] ... with Ansal Plaza ... detractors have ...
Ansal Plaza was a ... connection is u[n]...

110 I DARPAN I SEP-OCT 2006

SPONSORED FEATURE

that's not under us. Hudco is doing that.

Then you moved out to smaller towns in Uttar Pradesh, Punjab and Haryana.
About four years ago, as I saw Delhi expanding, I realised that spreading out horizontally was the only way the city could survive. The Metro Rail and the satellite townships are major steps in this spreading out process. But the satellites have to be well-planned, taking care of all civic amenities not only of the present but also of the future. The current mess of Delhi can be blamed on haphazard planning. When we moved out to two-tier towns like Sonepat, Panipat, Kurukshetra, Mohali, Jalandhar, Jaipur and Amritsar, we did so with meticulous planning. These towns did not have any planned townships. We successfully filled the gap. Right now we are building 15 such townships all over India. They are self-sufficient, luxurious and have own schools, clubs, malls and hospitals.

What's new in Delhi?
Here we are increasing the luxury quotient.

Like the Ivy at Gurgaon?
Yes. We are offering super-luxurious homes. As incomes increase and consciousness about global living standards rises, these luxury homes and clubs will be in great demand.

The Ansal group has also forayed into the hospitality sector.
We have developed many hotels like The Marriott but never get involved in running them. We work on a minority share basis. That suits us better. Next, we are coming up with a countrywide chain of heritage malls. These malls, built inside real palaces, will offer under one roof all the diversities of India's art and crafts. They'll sell handicraft items from all over the country in an air-conditioned environ. Best suited for the foreign traveller. The first one is at Rai Ka Bagh Palace in Jodhpur. The charm will be the old-world architecture that will remain untouched. To enhance the experience, Rai Ka Bagh will have winding streets and *bazaars*, colourful *baradari* and kiosks. One section will house the mall, while the other will have a spa and 50-100 service apartments.

Why not try infrastructure?
We haven't thought of exploring this sector though there are ample opportunities. The IT and BPO industries alone require 3-4 crore sq feet of developed area every year. We have tried it a little at the SEZ for glass and auto parts at Katputli while one more such industrial zone is being developed at Murthal.

We are not interested in building flyovers but are looking at developing ports, both sea and air. We are also researching the prospects of power generation.

Ansal was once the leader in real estate. But you have slipped.
We did suffer a little due to internal issues but now we are on a surge again. Last year, our annual turnover was Rs 800 crore and profit, Rs 180 crore.

Real estate, specially in Delhi and NCR, is witnessing an unexplained boom. Property prices have skyrocketed and various small players are mushrooming.
Right now even the small players are investing big. But they may not be able to survive in the long run. There are various speculative reasons jacking up property prices and these should settle down in a few years. But in the housing sector, the boom will continue. According to the books, no metropolis should have more than a 10 per cent gap in supply and demand in housing. Delhi needs about 2 million dwelling units at present and as population increases, even in 20 years we'll not be able to meet the needs. This is the right time to invest in property. India needs about Rs 400,000 crore to meet housing demands.

Where will this money come from?
From real estate mutual funds. As the chairman of the National Housing Committee of FICCI, I am pursuing the Centre to introduce Real Estate Investment Trust (REITS). This innovative method of collecting money from individuals and investing it in real estate is being successfully followed in America.

What about the complaint that Indian construction companies are not globally competent. Can they handle this kind of mass investment?
It is true but surprisingly when the same companies take up projects abroad they are super efficient. The problem is in faulty planning. We, unlike the Japanese, don't plan meticulously. The Japanese plan everything, right to the last nut and bolt. Though things are improving here.

Talking about offshore projects, Ansal was the first to get clearance to take up construction projects abroad.
Yes and we did a number of projects in Bangkok, Russia and Iran. Now it's Abu Dhabi and Dubai.

Any lessons learnt?
We picked up new technologies. We have learnt how not to have cost and time overruns.

What about corporate responsibilities?
We have built the most eco-friendly township, Aravalli Retreat. We even have UN certification "for it being the finest in environment upgradation."

Our educational body, the Chiranjiv Charitable Trust, found in the 70s, has set up professional institutes like AIHE, a constituent of Ansal Institute of Technology (AIT), Sushant School of Art and Architecture, and School of Applied Sciences. Students from here are sent abroad for further studies. We are running hospitals and a free dispensary.

Finally, what does Sushil Ansal do when he's not dreaming bricks and mortar?
(Laughs). Plays golf. I am an avid golfer and a travel aficionado. At home, I love playing with my grandchildren. The pool is my perpetual haunt during summer. I love a swim, with my drink on the poolside and sometimes even have my dinner there.

Do you eat out often?
I love *ghar ka khana*. Mostly vegetarian. But when we do eat out, I prefer Thai. I also love fish and Bengali sweets.

Favourite restaurants...
The Imperial Hotel, 360° at Oberoi, Geoffrey's (owned by daughter) and the South Indian fare at Marriott's Dakshin.

I love *ghar ka khana*. Mostly vegetarian. But when we do eat out, I prefer Thai and the South Indian fare at Marriott's Dakshin. And I can't resist fish and Bengali sweets

SEP-OCT 2006 I DARPAN I 111

explomedia
TO ADVERTISE
Hi

HERALDING RETAIL REVOLUTION

First shopping mall in Delhi 1999

ANSAL PLAZAS ALL OVER INDIA

GREATER NOIDA

JODHPUR

LUDHIANA

PALAM VIHAR

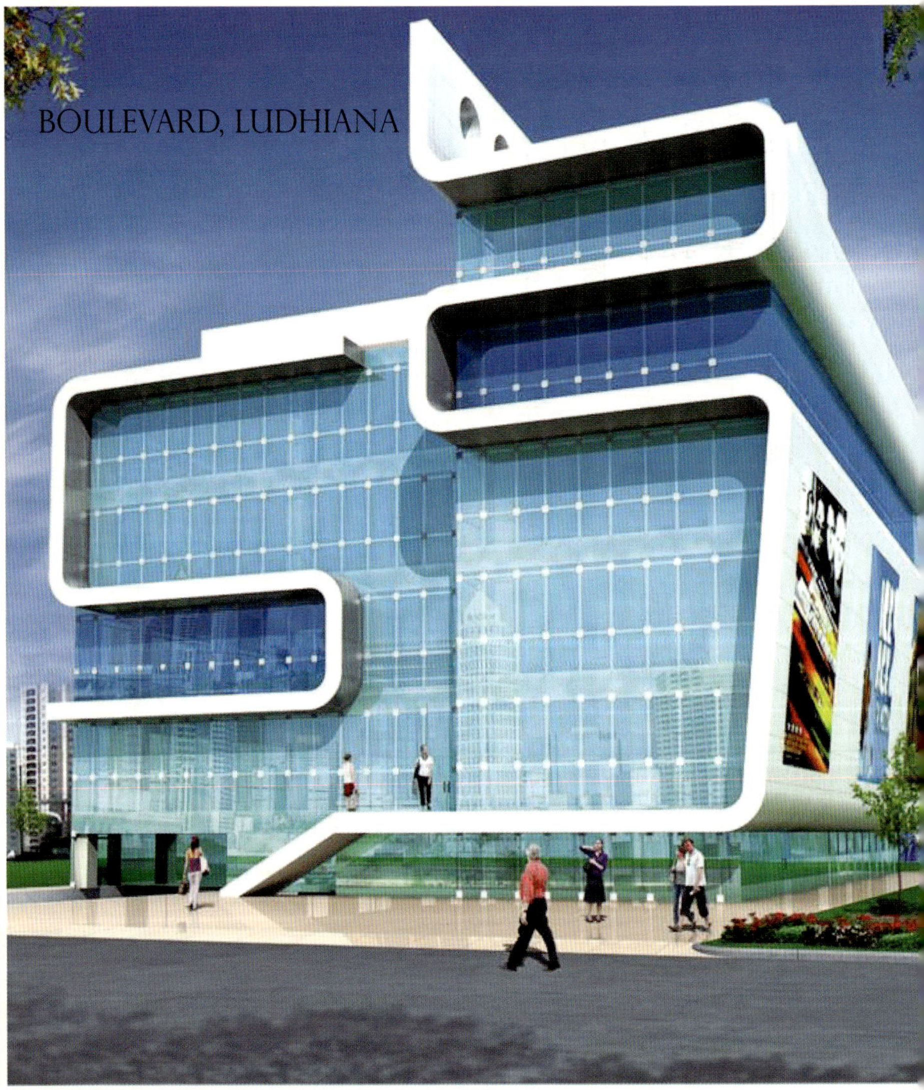
BOULEVARD, LUDHIANA

JALANDHAR

SONEPAT

FACE OF MODERN RETAIL

The Ansal Plaza brand name has been taken to various locations in north India

AWARDS

Facing page

■ JUST REWARD

Sushil receives an award from Salman Khurshid, now the Union Minister for Corporate Affairs

1987	Award given by Industries Association of Chandigarh
1987	Meridian Gold Award for best contribution in housing
1988	Shiromani Award for outstanding contribution in the housing and construction industry
1991- 1992	Overeseas Construction Council of India (OCCI) Award for maximum repatriation of foreign exchange in consultancy projects in the year
1992-1993	OCCI export Award for the second best performance in the category of maximum foreign exchange repatriated to India from overseas service contracts
1993	AIMO Visvesvaraya Entrepreneurship Award.
1993	Industrial Excellence Award
1999–2004	Award given for Invaluable contributions in building Credai.
2001	Delhi Factory Owners Association Award for outstanding contribution in the field of housing
2001	Award given by District Red Cross Society, Gurgaon
2003	Award given by National Real Estate Development Council for contributions towards 'Housing for All'
2006	Reader's Digest Award for Most Trusted Brand in Real Estate Industry
2007	Amity HR Excellence Award
2005- 2006	Building Industry Leadership Award.
2005-2006	Smart Living Award
2006	Lifetime Achievement Award given by Punjabi Parvasi Divas
2006	Young Icon Building Industry Leadership Award
2007	CW Top Builders Award.
2007	Building. Industry Leadership Award
2008	Leadership And Excellence Award given by Business & Economy (B&E) Magazine
2009	Distinguished Service Award Bestowed upon Ansal API (WCCPGC 2009).
2009	Edinbrugh Management Connection Queens Medallion for the year
2009	Star Retailer Award by Franchisee India Ansal for Ansal API's contributions in Retail Realty

PHASE FOUR

UPHAAR

When you bring up the Uphaar tragedy with Sushil, his face turns ashen. Fifty-nine people lost their lives on that fateful day. Shaking his head ever so slowly, his eyes revealing an inner pain, he is quick to correct, "not 59, but 60. A part of me also died that day. A decade and a half has passed, but this is a wound that time is unable to heal for those 59 innocent victims and their families that suffered. It is a grief I will carry with me to my grave. I and my family feel extremely sorry for the tragedy and have always shared the pain of the families who have lost their dear and near ones."

Derived from Latin, the expression "annus horribilis" translates to "horrible year". It was made famous by Queen Elizabeth II in her Christmas message in 1992 when she referred to the year about to end as "annus horribilis". It had been packed with sorrow: two of her sons had got divorced; her beloved Windsor Castle had suffered a big fire. Everyone has his or her own annus horribilis, the one eminently sorrowful year in a busy lifetime of everyday ups and downs. For Sushil, this was 1997. It was a twelve-month period replete with challenges and sadness, with personal and professional crises, with turbulence at work and at home, with health complications. Its biggest jolt was the Uphaar tragedy.

The year couldn't have begun on a harsher note. As 1997 dawned, the first round of India's economic reforms had spluttered to a conclusion. A weak coalition government comprising regional parties was ruling the country. Bereft of political and policy stability, the real-estate sector was coping with the additional burden of a crash in rates, particularly in key markets such as Delhi and Mumbai. Precisely because the boom that had preceded this crash had been unprecedented in its magnitude, the bust too was of momentous proportions.

Preceeding page
SILVER SCREEN
At its height, Uphaar was one of Delhi's best movie theatres

In the Ansal household, there were several concerns. An otherwise fit person, devoted to an early morning yoga session and a regular stint in his gym, Sushil had never known debilitating illness. Yet, in early 1997 he suffered repeated bouts of ill-health. The recurring fever and persistent cough defied diagnosis and a plethora of visits to doctors and medical tests did not seem to solve the mystery. Sushil began to weaken. "At one point," Kusum recalls, "he had lost almost twenty kilos and his appetite was gone. He could barely speak, his throat was so badly damaged."

Finally, when all available options failed, it was decided to move him to London for diagnosis and treatment. Here he was pronounced to be suffering from tuberculosis of the larynx. His lungs had been severely affected and he had to stay on for a few weeks for treatment. There was a lump on one of his lungs that had to be surgically removed and required a biopsy to establish whether it was malignant. Luckily, it was not. Given all this, it was only in April 1997 that Sushil and Kusum returned to India, despite his doctors' advice to postpone his departure and take complete rest. Sushil agreed to spend the rest of the summer in a hill station for his health.

On returning to India, plans had to be changed. Sushil's brothers, Gopal and Deepak, announced they were planning overseas vacations for extended durations. Kusum was taken aback but Sushil refused to ask his brothers to reconsider, not wanting to deny them family holidays that coincided with school breaks for their children.

It had always been this way. A workaholic, Sushil had spent his professional years without a well-defined sense of leisure for himself. Yet, he had always indulged his brothers, his children and nieces and nephews. Sushil was the older brother who always stepped up to the plate. As such, it was no surprise when Sushil brushed aside apprehensions about his health and did not interfere with Gopal's and Deepak's programmes.

Obviously, he could not spend the summer in a secluded hill station. In 1997, mobile phones had just come into the market. The Internet was very limited in its usage; email was not yet a common tool of business communication. Sushil realised that if he wanted to be in hourly touch with his office, talking to a range of managers and associates, he would have to be readily accessible and this was only possible if he stayed in Delhi.

In the middle of June 1997, Kusum and Sushil decided to fly down to Pune and spend time with their daughter Alpana and her husband, Rahul Kirloskar. "Rahul's grandmother had died some days earlier," Sushil says, "and we thought it appropriate to go down and pay our respects." It was at 4 p.m. on June 13 that Sushil and Kusum landed in Pune. "I remember we had some guests over from Chandigarh that day," Alpana says, "my parents entered the house and everybody was having tea. Then Pranav called ..." Father and son spoke for almost an hour. Pranav told him of the fire in Uphaar. A Delhi Vidyut Board (DVB) transformer located on the stilt floor of the movie theatre had sparked a fire and the rescue operations were on. Sushil's face darkened. "He was constantly on the phone," Rahul says, "and his instinct was to take the first flight back to Delhi. It was a sleepless night. He was very worried about the people in the cinema and made constant inquiries about the evacuation and rescue process."

The next morning Sushil and Rahul drove down to Pune airport. Rahul remembers that journey well. "He looked completely shattered," he says of his father-in-law. "He was thinking of nothing else. What had gone wrong, what could have been done to prevent it ... Those were the only things on his mind." The airport held further disappointment. June 14, 1997 was a Saturday, and Indian Airlines did not fly from Pune to Delhi on that day. India's private aviation expansion hadn't yet occurred so Sushil and Rahul had no option but to drive back home. Sushil was now expected to fly to Delhi on the earliest available flight.

From Pune, he called Gopal and Deepak and informed them about the sad tragedy. He asked his brothers to cancel their trips and rush back. Both perhaps did not realise the seriousness and declined. To Sushil, this was a shock. He was on his own.

Meanwhile, in Delhi the storm had burst. Vipin Luthra, Sushil's older son-in-law and Archana's husband, knows the details to this day. "My wife and children were travelling and towards the evening I decided to drop in at Nirula's for a snack," he says, "and that's when the phone call came." Vipin rushed to a control room that had been set up by senior staff members and began to do what he could. "Of course, I was in regular touch with Pune," he says, "we were on the phone till maybe 3 a.m."

Emotions were running high. At the same time neither Sushil nor any of his immediate family quite understood they would be held

What made matters worse for Sushil was going through the names of those who had died in the tragedy. So many were familiar – some were friends, others business associates.

responsible for the fire. As far as they could make out, it had been caused by DVB's equipment malfunctioning and Uphaar was a victim of external failure. However, it soon became clear not everybody saw it that way. "That day," Vipin says, recalling the precise moments when the implications of Uphaar began to hit him, "the police reached the homes of both brothers even before the ambulances reached the hospitals."

What made matters worse for Sushil was going through the names of those who had died in the tragedy. So many were familiar – some were friends, others business associates. One such family, the Sidhus, lived in Ashadeep. Sushil telephoned S.S. Sidhu, the head of the family and a friend, and his son Raman Sidhu, and expressed his condolences and sorrow. Kusum's brother Subodh and wife Purnima, who also lived in the same building, were requested to visit the Sidhus and Mr. R.S. Mann, whose wife had died, and help in whatever manner possible. They shared the pain and grief of the victims' families and helped them in whatever way they could. With the extended family chipping in – Pranav's father-in-law, Rajendra Miglani, flew down from Mumbai – "we tried to ensure at least one representative visited each bereaved family and shared their grief," says Vipin. Vinod, Kusum's brother who had just resettled in Delhi after returning from Bangkok was also concerned and helping the victims families.

Unfortunately everybody was busy in fault-finding. "We, on the other hand, were trying to reach out to the victims' families and provide all types of medical treatment and cure and rehabilitate them. This was given due priority," says Vipin. They expected ideas and solutions from every quarter to help the families of victims in this hour of need. "We could not have brought back those who left us but we were trying to walk an extra mile in whatever way which could console, comfort or mitigate suffering and pain. Unfortunately sometimes our help was being misunderstood and misrepresented," says Sushil.

As was only to be expected, the family members of those who had died were shattered, disconsolate and angry. The media frenzy had also begun. Unfortunately, the media did not interview senior executives at Uphaar to ascertain the facts and sequence of events. This led to lopsided reporting and a limited picture was presented to the public. The media campaign took the Ansals unawares. They were taken aback by the ferocity of the attack. "Since the matter was sub-judice, my dignified silence was perhaps used against me," says Sushil. They never did present their side of the story and nor was the media prepared to present it. The Ansals became the victims of a misdirected campaign, although they also only wanted justice. One should not pre-decide and prejudge the accused. It should have been left to the judiciary system and not influenced by media reports.

The failure of the DVB to maintain the transformer, install necessary protective relays, get mandatory approvals from the chief electrical inspector of Delhi and undertake adequate repairs was not reported in the manner it should have been. Senior functionaries of DVB were not under the media – or even police – gaze. Shortcomings on the part of other public agencies were ignored. The fire brigade was not equipped with sufficient water pumps, oxygen masks, hydraulic ladders and fire jackets. Ambulances did not have sufficient oxygen cylinders and first-aid facilities. The families of victims were unhappy with the medical care provided and the lack of sufficient beds, doctors, and life-saving medicines in the hospitals. Many lives could have been saved if the public agencies had performed their part. It was a system collapse. The depositions of some of the prosecution witnesses in the court bear this fact out very clearly and loudly.

Meanwhile the police process had started. Sushil arrived in Delhi to present himself for interrogation. "It began at 10 a.m. and concluded at 8 p.m. and answered all questions raised by police," he recalls of that gruelling day. Thereafter, he left for Bangalore and Mumbai for his treatment. During this period, Kusum and Sushil visited Shirdi and several temples, praying for the souls of those who had died, and for justice to be done to them. Unexpectedly Sushil was arrested in Mumbai. Surprisingly, they also arrested Sushil's son Pranav who had nothing to do with Uphaar.

On Sushil's and Pranav's arrest in 1997, dark clouds engulfed the Ansal household. Streams of relatives, friends and well-wishers visited Kusum and Sheetal to give them the strength and courage to face the ordeal. They reassured them that Sushil would be free soon. Kusum says "I was emotionally touched when I saw Neelam (Sheetal's mother) shift from Mumbai and handle the kitchen and household while Sheetal and I were in trauma. Rajendra Bhai Sahib came down from Mumbai

Ambulances did not have sufficient oxygen cylinders and first-aid facilities. The families of victims were unhappy with the medical care provided and the lack of sufficient beds, doctors, and life-saving medicines in the hospitals. Many lives could have been saved if the public agencies had performed their part

and spent most of his time in Delhi, consulting lawyers and advisors till Pranav was back." Sushil too recalls this. "How can I ever forget what he and Neelam and all our relatives and friends did for me and my family?" he says.

The public at large was surprised at Sushil's arrest. Sushil had resigned as director of Ansal Theatres and Clubotels a full nine years before the fire. He did not directly or indirectly run the theatre or supervise the day-to-day management of Uphaar. It didn't seem right to take into custody a former director after the accident. Yet, not only was Sushil arrested, so was Pranav – even though he had never been an employee of Uphaar's owner company. "At one point," says Sushil, "a police officer even threatened to arrest my 93-year-old mother." Ultimately Pranav's name didn't figure in the First Information Report (FIR)/Charge Sheet, but the innocent boy had to suffer unnecessarily. "Is the police or anyone accountable for such irresponsible action? Who will make good his suffering and trauma?" ask Sushil and Kusum. It was obvious the police had been satisfying a public hunger for "tough action."

Looking at the Uphaar tragedy, it is a wonder that while the Ansals were arrested and so were Uphaar's managers as well as minor DVB employees, not one senior civic or public utility official was either charge-sheeted or punished. Apart from a few very junior functionaries, nobody from the Municipal Corporation of Delhi (MCD), the DVB, the fire brigade and the range of other urban regulatory and monitoring authorities even had charges brought against. It is a clear case of the police once again showing bias against the private sector while in the eyes of the law there is no discrimination between public sector undertakings and the private sector in matters of criminal negligence. A hands on employee/manager/executive director, directly looking after operations, and directly responsible for criminal negligence should be held responsible in criminal law and not retired or not actively involved people. "This is the law," say most leading criminal lawyers.

In terms of human emotions and wrenching loss, every tragedy has a sameness to it. Yet, each tragedy is also specific: there is a cause, a reason for it, an underlying source of guilt. No doubt Uphaar too has to be assessed in this framework. To do so, however, would also require a study of the history and circumstances of the movie theatre, and how they may have contributed to Black Friday, June 13, 1997.

Take the cause of the fire. The fire was not triggered by any device under the control of the cinema but by a transformer that had been installed on the stilt floor of the building complex by the Delhi Electric Supply Undertaking (DESU, later renamed the DVB). Under Indian Electricity Rules, DESU had the right to take space from a bulk consumer in its premises for installation of their facility. In 1972, they took 375 square feet of space in Uphaar at a token amount of Rs. 11 per square feet per annum. This transformer was under the lock and key of DVB and was responsible for supplying electricity to the residents of the Green Park neighbourhood and to a few office spaces in the building, but not to Uphar cinema itself. Uphaar had its own transformer which supplied power to the theatre and is intact till now because it was well maintained and duly accredited by the chief electrical engineer of Delhi under the Indian Electricity Rules.

How well did DESU and its successors do their job? Consider the evidence given by K.L. Grover, electrical inspector, Government of Delhi, who inspected the "partially burnt" transformer on June 14, 1997, the day after the horrific fire. He found "loose connections," "cables ... lying in haphazard ways instead of being laid in the cable trenches as required," not covered "with non-flammable slabs to avoid the spread of fire." There was more: "Protection relays were missing and HT oil circuit breakers were not found provided with a protection system;" "the 1,000 kv transformer ... was not having sufficient clearances as required ... which would be 1.25 metres all around the transformer in the case of an enclosed room..." Grover's entire testimony points to many such "deviations" that resulted in a short circuit. In fact, the DVB had not received mandatory approval for the transformer from the Chief Electrical Inspector of the Delhi government and was supplying electricity unauthorisedly.

Thus the DVB transformer was the villain of Uphaar. Due to poor maintainance and faulty repair, the DVB transformer caught fire, igniting 850 litres of transformer oil and creating a river of fire which also burnt some patrons' cars in the parking area. It is little known that the Uphaar management filed a case against the DVB in the Delhi High Court, charging it with negligence that led to loss of human lives and damaged the cinema building and business. The court's verdict is awaited.

Uphaar at that time was one of the leading cinemas of south Delhi. It was most sought-after by film producers for premiere functions. It was also a venue for international film festivals. Its safety and conformity with contemporary cinema practices was of the utmost importance.

The number of seats in the hall was also a subject of speculation in terms of their compliance with safety provisions. This number too has an interesting history. In 1976, the Lieutenant Governor of Delhi issued a populist directive asking for prices of cinema tickets to be brought down by 10 per cent. In turn, over forty movie halls were allowed to increase seats. Uphaar was given permission to increase seats by 100. However, this notification was withdrawn in July 1979 and all cinemas were directed not to increase the seats.

The cinema owners' association moved the Delhi High Court. The High Court directed the licensing authority to inspect every cinema in Delhi and allow additional seats in compliance with the Delhi Cinematography Act and Rules, and till then, give temporary licences to cinemas. After the judicial order, the Uphaar management applied for approval. Following inspections, it was allowed to retain 38 of the 100 seats it had added. It duly complied with this order and got the approval of the licensing authority.

Other changes in the theatre, such as shifting exit doors and creating boxes and gangways, were permitted as per the rules and regulations of the Cinematography Act. All these were approved by the MCD, the Fire Department of Delhi and the licensing authority as they were found in compliance with the norms or not of much consequence. The cinema license was renewed at specified intervals. The licencee was not an individual but the owning company, and at the time of fire, the persons representing the company and obtaining approvals and dealing with the authorities were Mr R.M. Puri and Mr I.C.L. Malhotra

Indeed, Uphaar at that time was one of the leading cinema theatres of south Delhi. It was most sought after by film producers and actors for premiere functions. It was also a venue for international film festivals. Its safety and conformity with contemporary cinema practices was of the utmost importance and the safety precautions were enforced and practised.

While the lengthy trial was on and hundreds of witness were examined and old government records studied by the court, unfortunately the media kept on giving a biased picture of the tragedy. Sushil and Gopal were eventually convicted by a trial court in Delhi in 2007 for negligence.

On Sushil's and Gopal's conviction, the business community, Chambers of Commerce and Industries and Cinema Exhibition Associations and many sections of the society were shocked. How could the former directors of Ansal Theatres and Clubotels, the company that owned and managed Uphaar, be held responsible for the fire or the safety and well being of the patrons who visited the cinema, specially when all licenses and approvals were in place and renewed periodically after inspections by several agencies? Sushil had resigned in 1988, nine years before the fire, and did not have any share holding in the company. The company was managed by a professional board of directors and a team of senior executives well skilled in cinema management. This question still remains unanswered. "We did not imagine we would be held criminally liable for something in which we had no indirect or direct role. The necessary compensation as and when decided by the Court was paid by the cinema owning company to the victim, families. If a fire takes place in a factory, a hotel or office, then are the Managing Director or the Directors of the company put behind bars when the powers of day-to-day management and control are with senior officers? Will one put the Chairmen of the Railway Board or the Chairman of the Delhi Metro Corporation behind the bars, if people die due to a train collision?"

Sushil and Gopal appealed to the Delhi High Court and bails were granted. The famous criminal lawyer, Ram Jethmalani, while arguing in the High Court against the conviction of his clients showed disappointment at the persistent propaganda and unfounded thirst for revenge in the media which could lead to a miscarriage of justice. The High Court upheld the conviction but reduced the sentence from two years to one year. The terms of an Uphaar gatekeeper and of some DVB employees were reduced from seven to two years. The managers of Uphaar were acquitted. In regard to the Ansals and others, an appeal is now pending before the Supreme Court.

How could the former directors of Ansal Theatres and Clubotels, the company that owned and managed Uphaar, be held responsible for the fire or the safety and well being of the patrons who visited the cinema, specially when all licenses and approvals were in place and renewed periodically?

In September 2008, the bails of Sushil and Gopal were cancelled for reasons that still baffle legal luminaries and society at large. They faced false allegations of tampering and were arrested in a case for which even the trial had not begun. They were put in prison for almost four and half months (September 2008 to January 2009). Being sent off to Delhi's Tihar Jail in such a manner actually evoked a lot of surprise, shock and sympathy for Sushil and Gopal in legal and in business circles. Ram Jethmalani echoed the feelings and sentiments of many by saying "it is unprecedented and unheard that without any proper evidence or proof and without hearing the case on merits, merely on alleged revengeful complaint, the Honourable Court should cancel bail."

"Putting him back in jail in September 2008 was unfair," says Rahul. K.P. Singh of DLF, Sushil's old friend and competitor, was so upset that he called Kusum and said he wanted to visit Sushil in jail. "It was important to demonstrate solidarity," says Singh, explaining why he went to Tihar and met Sushil in the autumn of 2008.

"I am indeed emotionally touched by the thousands of messages and letters that I received from a cross-section of society expressing support and affection and giving me strength to face the undeserved ordeal" says Sushil.

Uphaar has been a part of Sushil's psyche for 13 years now. "It has affected our lives, our emotions as well as our business," he says, "it triggered the partition and restructuring of our business." Pranav came of age with Uphaar and grew ten years in that harrowing summer of 1997. He shakes his head and talks of the "sub-normal conditions" of that time: "I must have given a hundred television interviews on Uphaar. It drained me ... This is a scar we have to efface."

To Kusum, Sushil's four-and-a-half months in prison in 2008-09 were particularly traumatic because they came out of the blue and were seen as particularly undeserved. This was when the children took charge. Vipin stopped going to his office for a month and was constantly with the lawyers. Alpana came down to Delhi and got immersed in the case, doing the rounds of legal chambers and courts. Archana remembers being called by her mother's cook late in the evening one day in September 2008. Kusum hadn't eaten in three days and the cook was distraught. "It became my duty to go there every evening at about 8.30 and ensure she ate," says Archana.

Sheetal marvels at her father-in-law's spirit and confesses that in the darkest days of Uphaar, "he was the one who keep the family going." Vipin remembers the night before his surrender to the police in September 2008: "He seemed to be more worried about the effect it was having on others, and consoling his office executives and domestic staff. He even spoke to his grandchildren about school."

In Tihar, Sushil kept himself busy. A natural listener, he began to interact with fellow prisoners, many of them too poor to afford lawyers and behind bars for petty, poverty-related crimes or on suspect grounds. He became their advisor and he would spend hours consoling them and advising them. On more than one occasion, he asked his lawyers to organise legal support for some such prisoners. He also mobilised the prison community and put together a cultural event as permitted by the jail rules. He says it was his attempt to "generate a positive energy" and live life as it comes. He adjusted himself to the jail's rules and regulations, got used to the jail food, and slept on the floor, under a fan in the hot season. He read lots of books and reflected on his life. That was when he thought of writing his life story.

The Uphaar crucible was a test of friendships. Some old comrades, like K.P. Singh, K.S. Bains and Ram Jethmalani came out shining and Sushil will never forget them. Yet, a few failed. "Some of my literary friends did not call for months after Uphaar," Kusum says, "some people who had sought help or sponsorship from Sushil in earlier times had not a word of sympathy." There were honourable exceptions. Shobha Doctor, who had made a television series based on one of Kusum's books, came down from Mumbai and stood firm.

"Eventually," says Sheetal, "it just got us to prefer living private lives. Uphaar brought us so much publicity that it put us off the limelight." The media's role hurt. "I was clear it was an accident and he was not responsible," says Rahul, echoing what more than one member of the family says. "What was not to my expectation was the media trial and the rigours of the judicial process in the country. It was an eye-opener. It is scary for any businessman and demotivates entrepreneurial spirit."

Sushil acknowledges Uphaar has wounded him in several ways. "Emotionally the case has shaken my faith," he says, "I have always prided myself as being considered straightforward and not thought ill of ... Sometimes I wonder: am I paying for a past birth? The second time I went behind bars, my wife broke down and started questioning God. I felt terrible."

Deep down, Sushil believes his previous success proved his undoing and there was an unseemly media-driven campaign to target "big names," a reflection of what is called the tall poppy syndrome: "If the cinema had belonged to a less well-known person, people would have targeted the DVB and the hands-on management," he says. In this case the Ansal name became a magnet. For instance, even though the prosecution has charged Sushil for a lesser offence (of negligence) than some government officials and a gatekeeper who faced more serious charges , he is often described in media reports as the "main accused!"

What also left its impact was the unfairness in treatment of private and public entities. In the case of the private sector company, the owners, directors and even former directors were arrested and convicted. At the DVB, the chairman, directors and chief engineers were not proceeded against: only a fitter and a junior engineer were charged.

Business growth too was stunted. Till 1997, DLF and the Ansals were at par. Today, DLF is far ahead. "The Uphaar legal battle preoccupied me and my inner urge to expand in business was diluted," says Sushil, "I guess this happened to Gopal too. If there had been no Uphaar in my life, I would have been a more useful citizen to Delhi and to India. It was a big blow. I became cautious, my risk-taking spirit declined."

His goodwill didn't decline, however. At the height of the Uphaar crisis, the Ansals needed to pay an instalment to the Housing and Urban Development Corporation (HUDCO) for the land on which Ansal Plaza was to be built, on south Delhi's Khel Gaon Marg. The chairman was in prison; the company's future was being dissected and written off in the newspapers. As old bankers of the Ansals, the board of Punjab National Bank nevertheless took a decision to release the loan of Rs 40 crore to HUDCO, as had been agreed earlier. Rahul and his brothers also came forward with an additional loan of Rs 15 crore to meet the shortfall. This saved the Ansals' allotment. "At trying moments, it is such faith and goodwill that keeps you going," says Sushil, "Ansal Plaza, which triggered the mall culture in Delhi, would not have been there today but for this help."

But Sushil openly confesses "the trauma that victim's families have gone through is much bigger and more unredeemable than ours, though I and my family have also been suffering great pain and agony since that day. We also have children, brothers and sisters and are sensitive to human beings. Therefore, through our various Trusts *(see chapter 6)* we are reducing pain, healing people, providing medical facilities, educating the poor and uplifting the underprivileged section of the society. This gives me solace, and peace and useful purpose in life." says Sushil.

Actually, the brothers sparked the most meaningful sub-plot of the Uphaar episode. In seeking a break-up of the joint family, they actually helped Sushil reappraise and appreciate his own nuclear unit. This was the collateral blessing from his annus horribilis.

Sushil still awaits redemption from Uphaar. He hopes the Supreme Court will do him justice when it decides on his appeal. Even so, he remembers many of the demons of 1997. "The word I love using for him," says Sheetal, "is 'resurrect.' You write him off and he resurrects. He had TB when he was arrested, his brothers abandoned him, there were financial problems and there was Uphaar. He still came back and grew the business and kept up with his social service activities." Rising from the ashes, Sushil to his family, friends and society at large, in Sheetal's words, is like the phoenix.

'A numb stillness prevails in my heart'

In November 2008, Sushil was in Delhi's Tihar Jail for what family and friends felt was a collateral and completely unfair charge related to the Uphaar case. At this point Kusum, best at expressing herself and her feelings in the written word, put down a long and emotionally wrenching letter to her husband. It is reproduced below.

Dear Sushilji,

I don't know how to express my feelings. I could never imagine this situation arising in our life. To read your name in the newspapers, with the added adjective of 'main accused', and then to see you behind those ugly, rusted bars ... It is nerve-racking. My feet shake and my heart cries when I stand in a queue, along with the relatives of various criminals, and undergo a personal security check. When someone asks me, 'Who do you have inside?' I press my lips. My heart cannot accept that a person such as you suffers these conditions. All your life you have worked hard with determination to reach business and professional success, adhering to moral and business ethics. I remember you took your brothers, hand-in-hand, to success in life. How much you trusted people, especially your brothers, but perhaps now is the time to learn some harsh lessons: 'Never ever trust, even those who you feel are close to your heart.'

Old images flash past as I try and analyse our life, your life. How simple you were ... always welcoming people with open arms, believing in giving, caring and sharing. You possess remarkable humility and have no ego. I know you would never dream of harming anybody. That's why my whole being is torn, as I see you on the other side of the wall. I can't even guess what discomfort and emotional turmoil you are going through. We don't get enough time to talk to each other; there are always so many people around.

During one of my visits you told me you had adjusted to 'this life.' I was left stunned, my innermost wounds hurt. I wondered how one could 'adjust to this life.' Is it adjustment to defeatism? But I believe in you, you are remarkably strong and brave,

PENSIVE

A writer first and foremost, Kusum has always expressed her emotions best when using pen and paper

because within you your conscience is clear and pure. You have not done anything wrong, intentionally or unintentionally.

Sushilji, sitting alone, in your quieter moments, I am sure you are thinking of how to address this double-edged unfairness. The major concern is whether the judiciary will be fair to you. Or will the interpretation of the media overpower the law, and deny justice? My heart beats faster and faster when I see the television coverage ...

It's been weeks since you've been away. Our Diwali was dark and full of tears. Even the children, Ayush and Anushka, sense the gravity. They don't say anything but don't want to hear about you or see television. My Karva Chauth was spent in the spell of sleeping pills, though my friends tried to support and cheer me.

When I visited you the other day, with a bag of the simple foodstuff permitted under jail rules – which one Hindi newspaper described as 'luxuries' provided to you – I watched from a distance as you handled business matters and spoke to Pranav and Vipin. When my turn came, you were exhausted and breathless. You were not allowed even a glass of water ... I could feel you were bottling up emotions, when you told me that though you do share a room with Gopal and a few others, there is no bonding despite living under the same roof for weeks.

Can you visualise those days of my life when I entered your family as a newly-married bride? You made it clear your parents and two brothers were your top priority. I adopted them like my own sisters and brothers and did whatever I could. I cooked food, nursed them when they were ill, with sincere honesty from my heart. I don't even remember how many days I spent in hospital rooms, nursing Indira, Meenakshi, Ritu or Divya during their deliveries or surgeries. Months and years I spent looking after Bhabiji [Sushil's mother]. Can you look back to see how much I neglected my own children, their simple needs, and sacrificed my own desires, dreams and my passion for life at that young age?

But today let me make a blunt confession, I feel I was cheated, a large segment of my life wasted cruelly for an insensitive family. I wonder how people can be so blind, not to see true love and sacrifice. Today I feel less of a person; a numb stillness prevails in my heart. I could have ended my life in disgust, but my children, grandchildren, my brothers, sisters in law, Neelamji and Rajendra Bhai Saheb and sincere friends are my strongest support. Without them I cannot survive this dark crisis. In fact, there are times when suicidal emotions threaten to overpower me.

The other day you asked me how I was. The truth is I don't have adequate words to describe where my heart is leading me to. All I can say is my life has become as twisted as a complex labyrinth. We are circling around the lawyers, desperately seeking legal advice. Everything seems so complicated and full of lies and inadequacies. I do attend most of the meetings with Pranav and Vipin, sometimes even go to court to listen to the hearings. When we come back, all of us, Alpana, Sheetal, Archana and I, cry. I don't know when this ordeal will end.

Well, it will give you some solace to know that I have organised a sudarshan puja, as Swamiji had suggested. It is a special 'repentance ritual' performed by Vedic priests and will last thirty days. Even though we are not guilty, let some kind of prayaschit [penance] happen. Maybe it is needed. Let us confess our sins, if there are any, before God. Sometimes I think our utmost sin was to love the people around us.

I am sure the power of these rituals and our pure spirit will provide certain kinds of vibrations of philosophical resonance, as our religion tells us. Please, every morning do spread your palms in front of God and receive his blessings. I am sure they will reach you. I am sure the sounds of mantras will whisper in your ears that everything in this world and life is ephemeral, that nothing lasts forever. That 'this too shall pass...'

Kusum

'I don't want my legacy marred by a tragic accident for which I was not responsible'

On October 7, 2008, Sushil wrote a letter to all his colleagues at Ansal API from Tihar Jail in Delhi. A very emotional letter that he drafted in his own hand, it was the outpouring of a decade of anguish and sense of hurt following the Uphaar tragedy of 1997. The letter is reproduced below.

Dear Ansal API staff members,

I thank you all for your support, understanding and for standing by me in this hour of crisis. It is in times like this that the true strength of character of a person emerges.

I was born in a simple middle-class family, with values of honesty, hard work and a spirit of nationalism. Thankfully these values have stayed with me. I recall the final day of my college life when I walked out of the examination centre at St Stephen's College to find my father waiting to take me to my life's first assignment, without any reprieve after my examination. I was taken straight to Hapur, where he was building a grain storage facility as a contractor, and from there started my working life. My father put me in charge of the work at Hapur and returned to Delhi. I used to live at the site, a few miles outside Hapur, in one room with a tin roof and a pedestal fan. In summers the tin roof and hot breeze made the room like an oven, which I did not mind as that was my training period. Living, eating and playing with my colleagues of all levels was part of my starting a career. Life carried on and it was never smooth sailing. Every time I fell, I got up bruised, but more determined and better prepared.

Nothing has affected my life more than the Uphaar tragedy. Not a day or night of my life has passed in the last twelve years without being haunted by the memories of that tragic accident. And contrary to what people may say, the horrific tragedy that befell all those who lost their precious ones was shared by me and my family too.

Ultimately, all of us have to answer to the highest court of all, and in that court, there is no prosecution and no defence. There is only oneself and one's maker, and I am at peace with my maker. My conscience is clear. I did not do anything to cause this tragic accident, in which 59 precious lives were lost. My own children, grandchildren, nieces and nephews were the most frequent visitors to the cinema. Why would my brother or I wish to harm or hurt anyone? I have spent my life helping people, be it my friends, relatives, business associates or employees.

Though I have not directly or indirectly contributed to the loss of 59 precious lives, I do want to be responsible to make and change the lives of as many children as possible who

LOST IN THOUGHT

The Uphaar trauma made Sushil reappraise his priorities

would otherwise be destined to live in misery and poverty. And this is something I will give shape to upon my release.

Many of the lives could have been saved had timely medical facilities and aid been available. Even reputed centres of medical excellence such as AIIMS [the All India Institute of Medical Sciences, New Delhi] and Safdarjang Hospital were not prepared for such a large rush of people. They were short of oxygen, doctors and even beds to meet such an emergency. Even the fire brigade was not equipped with gas masks and safety nets as they should have been. The equipment of the fire tenders, such as suction pumps, was not in working condition.

I have few regrets in life, the major one being that I followed the advice of my advisors and well wishers, against my own better judgment, and did not stand with the victims of this horrific tragedy in their hour of grief. That has turned out to be one of the biggest mistakes in my life. By the time I was released from custody on bail, the atmosphere had turned so hostile, and any contact with the victims may have been viewed by the court as trying to win over witnesses, that I again abstained from doing so.

As many of you know, at the time of the tragedy I had just returned from the United Kingdom after an operation and was recovering from tuberculosis, and had planned to be with my daughter in Pune for a few days to rest and recuperate from my ailment. During the period following the tragedy, my wife and I spent days visiting religious shrines in Shirdi, Tirupati and other places to pray for the departed souls and seek peace for the victims' families.

The business that we run today has had the benefit of the support of each one of you and of your families. I am grateful for that. Each one of you, my colleagues, has been instrumental in this journey. In normal cases, this business would have evolved and I would have had more time to not just induct my son Pranav but also to guide him. I have now decided that it is best if Pranav runs the business. I have full faith in his leadership and I would like all of you to extend to him your fullest cooperation as you have been doing to me. You have all been my strength and I hope you will work with Pranav to not only tide over this crisis and keep the flag flying but also to raise the business to new heights.

In doing so, you must all commit yourselves to the highest standards of corporate governance. The colonies and the buildings that we build must be safe well beyond the standards demanded by the regulatory authorities. These must be green and environmentally-friendly and must be the best. You and the country should be proud of them.

Over the last few days, my family has received thousands of calls and messages meant for me, showing support and affection, and for that I am very grateful. The last twelve years have been the most difficult period of my life. I am not overly concerned about the physical discomforts that one has to endure when being in jail. Back in Hapur, my only entertainment after a hard day's work used to be my late night visits to the Hapur railway station where I could read the magazines and books at the Wheeler & Co. bookstall without having to buy them, and watch trains come and go with hundreds of people from different walks of life arrive and depart. I also spent many years of my life in Gorakhpur, with my wife and young children, where I built the fertiliser factory as a contractor with very limited resources. I had to rely on loans taken from local shopkeepers to fund the construction work for the project. When I used to receive payments of my bills, I would go and pay the shopkeepers back with interest, only to take a loan again the very next day from the very same shopkeepers.

I started work when I was just eighteen. I am 69 today. I have invested fifty years of my life building a reputation and a business based on honesty, ethics and good business practices. I do not want these fifty years of hard work to go in vain. I do not want my legacy marred or marked by this very tragic accident for which I was not responsible. Money or power never have been nor are my personal priorities. Though I would have liked to live the rest of my life in peace and dignity, the damage to my reputation and legacy can only be undone by my devoting time and energies for the good of society. Upon being released from jail I will not go back to actively looking after the business and shall leave this responsibility to Pranav. I shall be available for guidance only on policy issues and shall head the Corporate Social Responsibility initiative.

We have in the past, as a part of our CSR programme, built and run schools, colleges and dispensaries, provided aid, land and building for old age homes; and funded and subsidised education. While continuing with these initiatives, the focus of our CSR will be to build for the underprivileged. I still have the strength, energy and will to work twelve to fourteen hours a day and I hope I will live long enough to build thousands of homes in different states by working with state governments on a 'no profit, no loss' basis for the weaker sections of society. We will seek the participation of other eminent persons and institutions in this initiative. We will bring new technologies to India so a home can be constructed in four days.

I want you all to hold your head high. I have done no wrong. We have done no wrong. We have been the victims of perhaps a misdirected campaign against us for the last twelve years which we have fought and will continue to fight. Have faith in God. I am confident that justice will finally prevail. I want each one of you to keep the faith. I have the fullest faith in God and in our judiciary. I know justice will ultimately be done. And for that day I fervently pray. Please convey my love and best wishes to each of your family members.

With best wishes,
Sushil Ansal

PHASE FIVE

THE FAMILY ANCHOR

Lala Maya Dutt
Wife Radha Rani

- Lala Hans Raj, Wife Sanchi Devi
- Ram Rakha Mal
- Bhagwanti Devi
- Bharti Devi

Lala Hans Raj, Wife Sanchi Devi:

- Durga Vati
- Lala Chiranji Lal (Married to Suraj Kumari)
- Prasanni
- Yasodah

Lala Chiranji Lal (Married to Suraj Kumari):

- Shiela Married to Om Prakash sarin
- Leela Married to Baldev Krishan Abbi
- Sushil Married to Kusum
- Indra Married to Rajinder M. Puri
- Meenakshi Married to Ashok Verma
- Gopal Married to Ritu
- Deepak Married to Divya

Gopal Married to Ritu:

- Suruchi
- Shewta

Deepak Married to Divya:

- Kushagra
- Karun

Sushil Married to Kusum:

- Archana Married to Vipin Luthra
- Alpana Married to Rahul Kirloskar
- Pranav Married to Sheetal

Archana Married to Vipin Luthra:

- Sukriti
- Abhishek

Alpana Married to Rahul Kirloskar:

- Alika
- Aman

Pranav Married to Sheetal:

- Ayush
- Anuska

No appraisal of Sushil Ansal can be complete without seeing him in the context of his family. The reference here is not just to his immediate family ~ Kusum and their three children ~ but to the extended family. Whether with his father, who influenced him in his earliest years, or his two sons-in-law and one daughter-in-law, all three of whom share a remarkably individual relationship with him, or his brothers, now estranged in personal and professional terms but brought up and reared almost as his own children, Sushil's bonds with members of his family have always been absolute.

For Sushil, the family was a large, expansive and indivisible entity. That is why it took the shock of Uphaar, and of his younger brothers demanding their share and essentially opting out, for him reappraise his relationships and focus more deeply on his own unit ~ the wife and children he had always seen as the equals of Gopal and Deepak and their families and not an ounce more precious.

Perhaps even without realising it, Sushil has been an inspiration for numerous others and is among the handful of veterans who more or less incubated the real estate development industry in India. Ramesh Chandra, the founder and doyen of Unitech, recalls their first meeting. "This is in 1970; Unitech was not in the real-estate business then. As structural engineering consultants, we were promoting the use of a new type of steel in construction. And we met Sushil Ansal in that context. I was very impressed at that meeting. I found him a straightforward and thinking man."

A decade and a half later, Unitech decided to diversify into real-estate development. In 1985, Chandra says, "I had only two models before me: Sushil Ansal and K.P. Singh." Happily all three "competitors" became close friends and collaborated in trying to free real-estate development from the maze of regulations that had enmeshed it. In doing this, they become personally wealthy, but also created much greater social wealth and made millions of families first-time homeowners.

Preceding page, bottom left
A DIVINE BLISS
(left to right): The grandshildren, Sukriti, Abhishek, Anushka, Aman, Ayush

Preceding page, bottom right
WITH GEN NEXT
(left to right): Pranav, Vipin, Sheetal, Alpana, Rahul, Archana

Preceding page, top
LIFE IS A VOYAGE
Kusum and Sushil have gone through so much together

Above
EARLY YEARS
Swinging moments: In the back garden of the Panchsheel Park house

It does seem strange that for an astute and intelligent businessman, one given to making fine distinctions and reading between the lines, Sushil never even considered the idea of individual ambitions and of his brothers wanting to move away and set up their own companies. As Rahul puts it, "If Uphaar hadn't happened, the family wouldn't have broken up in this generation." Despite the differences that have come up, Sushil still acknowledges the contribution of Gopal, who worked with him from 1972 to 1997, and Deepak, who was with him from 1977 to 1997. "They helped me build this company," he says, speaking from his heart.

Kusum still remembers a rather innocuous but telling inference she drew from a company brochure in the early 1990s: "It had pictures of the three brothers, but there was no mention of Pranav or me, although I was running the education end of the Ansal Group." If the idea of succession planning had entered Sushil's head before 1997, he clearly hadn't shared it. Archana puts it succinctly: "For Dad, it was always obvious that Gopal chacha would take over after him. The

chain of command extended to his brothers and only then to his son and the next generation." As she confesses, he was so busy with his role and obligations as a family patriarch that she sometimes "missed him as a pure father."

This was not surprising. For most of his life, Sushil saw himself as not the head of a nuclear family but as the guardian of a larger clan, comprising his brothers and sisters and their families, and an extended network of cousins, relatives and close compatriots of the Ansals. This was a mantle he had inherited from his father. At one level, Chiranji Lal (who died on March 1, 1983, at the age of 77, when Sushil was 44), was very different from Sushil. The father was impatient; the son is calm and rarely loses his cool. This contrast was among the first things Kusum noticed when she married into the Ansal family: "Sushil speaks firmly but never loses his temper. In fact, Sushil has made me a calmer person. My father-in-law was very different."

This ability to keep his cool has been remarked on, not just by family members, but professional associates as well. M.L. Soni, president

INDIA'S EXCLUSIVE MAGAZINE FOR COMPANY DIRECTORS, PRESIDENTS & VICE-PRESIDENTS

DIRECTOR DIGEST

VOL NO. 4 NO 6 | A ROSS MURARKA PUBLICATION | JULY 1985 | PRICE RS 8

TOWNSHIPS
The new real estate trend
DLF & Ansal lead the way

C.H. Raghavendra Singh, Chairman D.L.F.

Sushil Ansal, Chairman, Ansal Group

LIC plans mobilisation of funds in new areas

General Motors swings the biggest ever non-oil merger

Singhanias' commitment to societal obligations

Above

DINNER TIME

Kusum and Sushil with their then unmarried children in the Panchsheel Park house

Inset

THE DOYENS

On the cover page of a magazine, with Chaudhary Raghuvendra Singh, the founder of DLF

(taxation) at Ansal API, has been a colleague of Sushil's since 1969. He says of his boss: "He has a remarkable ability to control anger even in excruciating circumstances. He will not let it show. I don't believe there is no anger; it's just that he sublimates it and channels it positively. He backs people and motivates them at work – he doesn't coerce them by shouting." Meenakshi Varma, Sushil's youngest sister, says, "Because of our father's temper, we were a little wary of approaching him as children. We were freer with Sushilji. He was always a gentleman and we would go to him for help. He is a counsellor for not just me but my children as well."

Even so, there was a lot Sushil learnt from his father: a sense of duty, an exacting discipline in personal life, the belief that business was not just about money but part of a larger social calling. As he grew as a contractor, Chiranji Lal began to think in terms of what is today called corporate social responsibility. "He set up the Human Welfare Mission that ran free libraries and adult education centres in jhuggi-jhopdi (slum) colonies in Delhi as early as the 1960s," Sushil remembers. This left an impression on the young man, who often worked on such projects. Chiranji Lal also saw himself as responsible for not just his family but

EARLY YEARS

An old family picture: (Left to right): Sushil, his mother, sisters Leela and Indira and brother Gopal

distant relatives including those who came to him from his native village seeking a job, monetary assistance or any form of help. Sushil absorbed these attributes almost unconsciously.

It was an unusual upbringing. Chiranji Lal was not a very demonstrative man but loved and had high expectations of his son. Early in life, he had lost family members to malaria. Health was an obsession with him. He stayed away from tea and coffee, was strictly vegetarian and practised naturopathy. Sushil imposes no such restrictions on himself. However, he does exercise every morning, without exception, and for this too he must thank his father. "Bawji was a great advocate of yoga," he says, "every morning, at about 4 am, we used to drive to a yoga ashram in the Ridge area, just behind Birla Mandir. We used to carry our own chattais, I remember. I learnt yoga under the stars."

A man of unusual personal integrity, Chiranji Lal was Sushil's first role model. "His was a journey from near-poverty to comfortable middle-class status, from village life to city life," assesses Sushil, "he built the base for me." Grateful for this, Sushil began to see his siblings and their well-being as his natural duty. In a sense, he was trying to live up to his father.

Above
FITNESS FREAK
Working out at home

Inset
A SOLEMN RITUAL
In the puja room at home

Sushil was very close to his mother, Bhabiji, being the first surviving son of the family. He looked after her, especially after his father passed away. She was a very religions woman and performed many Hindu rituals, something Kusum was not accustomed to, as she came from an ardent Arya Samaji family. Bhabiji was fond of all her brothers and sisters which kept the families closely knitted together. She shifted to the Panchsheel Park house with Sushil and Kusum, staying with them till she passed away in October 2000. Sushil was with a business delegation in Korea when he heard the sad news and rushed back to Delhi. Till today, he can not overcome the regret that he was not by her bedside when she passed away. "It was very sudden. We all loved her very much and kept feeling her absence for many years," he says. He still remembers both his parents fondly and misses them.

When it came to his brothers, the age difference between them also played a role. Gopal and Deepak are nine and fourteen years younger than Sushil respectively. Chiranji Lal was not much interested in business during the later part of his life, due to his prolonged illness and Bhabiji had handed over the responsibility of managing the house, so Sushil and Kusum practically brought them up. The brothers were also fortunate that somebody was thinking of their future careers and attempting to fit them into a structure. Sushil had already done the spadework. "I was an economics graduate," he says, "but as our construction business grew, we needed family expertise on the technical side as well. I goaded both Gopal and Deepak to do civil engineering."

The division of responsibility was clear. Sushil was the chairman and managing director of the group of companies, responsible for commercial and financial decisions and for corporate strategy. He was also the public face of the Ansals. Gopal looked after the execution of projects. Shortly after graduating, Deepak was asked to take charge of a paper mill set up in Sikandrabad (Uttar Pradesh). The plant was inaugurated by the Chief Minister, N.D. Tiwari, in September 1976.

THOSE WERE THE DAYS
With brothers Gopal (extreme right) and Deepak (extreme left) and son Pranav at a family function

Deepak worked hard at the paper mill but felt there were better rewards in the real estate sector. The mill was, therefore, sold to Ashok Goel of Rampur Distilleries in 1989 and Deepak too moved into the family business of property development.

To neutral observers and family friends, it was always clear that Sushil was shielding his brothers and taking on a larger part of the business burden. Yet, obviously Deepak and Gopal (particularly the former) did not see it that way. There were latent ambitions and a desire to move away from Sushil's shadow. Perhaps this would have happened in the natural course of time. It was the impetuousness and timing that took Sushil by surprise. Shortly after getting back from his vacation in the summer of 1997, with the Uphaar controversy still raging, Deepak and his wife Divya mooted a partition. Sushil was stunned at the suggestion; the timing was most inappropriate. Initially Gopal and Ritu were not in favour of the partition, but could not convince Deepak and Divya. The inevitable happened.

Divisions take place in a number of business families, but Sushil regretted the absence of a family elder who would make his brothers see reason. He remembers telling Kusum one evening that if Divya's father, the late C.L. Anand – at one time the chairman of Toshiba-Anand – had been alive, the partition would not have taken place, at least not in the manner it did.

The brothers asked for equal division of not only the Ansal Group's assets and liabilities but also personal assets. This was absolutely contrary to the Chiranji Lal's will and expressed intentions. Sushil had put in sixteen years of work before Deepak joined the business and eleven years before Gopal joined. As the one who had built the company, he was entitled to a bigger share and this was the situation till the partition. However, so as to maintain peace in the family and to settle matters amicably – and to avoid prolonged litigation – Sushil agreed in principle to divide the business into three equal parts. Accordingly, all the business and personal assets of the family were pooled together. However, it was obvious Sushil was contributing most to this pool, as he had more shares in the companies as well as greater personal

SISTER MEENAKSHI'S WEDDING

Kusum with (left to right) Sheila behenji, Indira Puri, Meenakshi Verma and Leela behenji

VED AND VIMLA LUTHRA
Archana's in-laws are friends of the Ansals and from a prominent business family in Delhi

assets. Recognising this, Deepak and Gopal originally agreed to transfer properties of certain value to him personally, to partially compensate him for a three-way division. This never actually happened.

Three mediators valued the assets of the Ansal family and split them into three equal lots. T.R. Tuli and S.L. Chopra, both former chairmen of the Punjab National Bank and D.N. Davar, former chairman of IFCI, were chosen as mediators. When Tuli died midway through the process, he was succeeded by Hari Mitter, a well-known chartered accountant. All four gentlemen had known the Ansal family for years. They gave their awards in two instalments, in April and December 1999. The flagship company, Ansal Properties and Infrastructure (API), went to Sushil and so did all the major loans and liabilities of the group. Ansal Buildwell with projects in Gurgaon, Bangalore and Cochin, came to Gopal's share. Ansal Housing and Construction, with projects in Mumbai, Bhopal and Uttar Pradesh, went to Deepak.

Most of the debts, liabilities and intricate income tax legacies went to Sushil's share. It was decided that loans would be repaid from the proceeds of the common pool of properties. If sufficient funds were not generated from the common pool, the shortfall would be made up in equal measure by all three brothers. However, due to the economic slowdown in that period, selling the properties was not remunerative. Deepak and Gopal did not chip in with their share towards the repayment. The entire responsibility fell on Sushil and Pranav.

It was a testing time. In order to avoid default, Sushil pledged his personal properties – including his houses in Panchsheel and on Feroze Shah Road – and sold his farmhouse and a few other assets to honour pre-division commitments to the banks. He was already struggling with the Uphaar case and the recession in the real-estate business. Taking on the entire burden of repaying loans was an additional headache. However, Pranav and he strove to rebuild the company. Slowly the property market began to recover, and Sushil was able to pay off all loans and gradually release his personal properties from the banks. He was free again and ready to run the next leg of the marathon.

Sushil was now making a fresh start. However, more than the professional and financial obstacles, it was the emotional injury that stayed with him. The sense of loss, almost betrayal, by those he had nurtured as delicately as a gardener tends to his saplings was hard to

digest. Though he doesn't admit it, it probably still hurts deep inside. Indira Puri, Sushil's younger sister, talks of how the differences between her brothers devastated her: "We tried not to take sides. But frankly, Sushilji had done so much for us and for the entire family, he had been such a father figure, it was impossible not to sympathise with him."

Sushil had spent a lifetime being a giving person, always eager to help. He never let on, but in those low moments in the late 1990s, he had a right to feel cheated. As Rahul, his younger son-in-law, puts it, "I first met him in 1987. I found him a warm, caring and loving person... the sort who would gather people around him and lead. My instant judgement was that this was a very giving person."

So "giving" was Sushil that it astonished and sometimes perturbed Kusum that not only were his own interests not a priority, even those of his immediate family took second place. In 1982, a young man, Vipin, the son of Vimla and Ved Luthra, friends of Kusum's and Sushil's, paid him a sales call. He was attempting to sell computers, which were scarcely known in Indian offices at that point. Sushil heard him out and asked

THE LITTLE GIRL GROWS UP
Archana and Vipin Luthra's engagement

SUSHIL AND KUSUM WITH ARCHANA'S FAMILY

Archana, Vipin, Sukriti, Abhishek

THE CHANCELLOR CLUB, GURGAON

Sushil sees social and leisure infrastructure as crucial to the rich life of his new colonies

lots of questions but, as Vipin remembers with a smile, "didn't buy anything." He was impressed enough by the visitor to come home and mention him to Kusum as a likely match for the daughter of a relative. At this point, a friend decided to be blunt with Sushil and told him that Archana, his first child, had reached marriageable age and rather than just worry about nieces and nephews, maybe he should think about his own children as well!

The message got home. Shortly afterwards Archana and Vipin got married. Vipin's father had built Televista, a leading Indian electronics brand in the 1970s and early 1980s. By the 1990s, technology and competition had overtaken Televista and Vipin found himself in a crisis. It was at this stage that Sushil became, to quote Vipin, "more of a father than a father-in-law." "I had his implicit emotional, financial and practical support. He even gave me guidance, whenever needed, on negotiating with banks and financial institutions."

FUN TIME
At a family holiday in Pahalgam with his first grandchild, Sukriti

Vipin came out of the ordeal and today runs a successful hospitality business. He has also made substantial investments in real estate and the equity market. One of his companies is linked to the Ansals and he has promoted many clubs and resorts – including The Palms in Sushant Lok and the Chancellor Club in Palam Vihar, both in Gurgaon. Indeed, Vipin's luxury recreational and entertainment facilities are now seen as integral to new Ansal townships. With Ansal API, he has tied up with Gaj Singh, the former Maharaja of Jodhpur, to convert the Rai ka Bag Palace into a heritage hotel. He is also building world-class clubs in Lucknow's Sushant Golf City and in Megapolis, on the outskirts of Delhi.

Above
TEEING OFF
A keen sportsman from his school days, Sushil is golf obsessed

Inset
GOLFING TRIO
With Tejendra Khanna, presently the Lieutenant Governor of Delhi, the Japanese Ambassador to India and Ravi Wig

Rahul had lost his father, Chandrakant Kirloskar, as a boy and was brought up by his grandfather, S.L. Kirloskar (1903-1994). In theory,

this relationship was a great gamble. The Ansals and Luthras knew each other, both being Punjabi families in Delhi. The Kirloskars were Maharastrians based in Pune, where Rahul lived. It was a far cry from Delhi. Rahul's brother, Atul, had married a Delhi girl, Arti, the daughter of Shivraj Gupta, Sushil's "golfing buddy." In Delhi on a holiday, he met the Ansals, was instantly attracted to Alpana and they got married in 1988. Today, Alpana is very much a Pune person, fluent in Marathi and a successful architect and interior decorator. What strikes Rahul is the similarity between the families. "The credo is the same," he says, "stay away from the spotlight, be straight and honest in your dealings."

As it happened, Sushil and the senior Kirloskar got on famously, playing golf, discussing business and finding they both worked hard but, as individuals, weren't necessarily obsessed with money. The Kirloskar patriarch was a man of lofty ideas and impeccable business ethics. Sushil was both impressed and inspired by him. At the wedding, as per tradition, Sushil handed over the *shagun* in the form of money in an envelope and

Inset
TYCOON TRIO
In conversation with S.L Kirloskar and Rahul Bajaj

Above
THE KIRLOSKARS
At Alpana's wedding reception in Pune

some other gifts to Mothababa, as S.L. Kirloskar was called by his near and dear ones. Sushil tells the rest of the story: "After the *shagun* ceremony, he called me and returned the envelope, saying 'Sushil, you know I do not touch unaccounted money.' I told him 'Sir, it is from my personal bank account and fully accounted for.'

'Will you give an affidavit on oath' he enquired. I replied, 'yes!' Only with a lot of persuasion did he retain the envelope. It is rare to come across people of such high integrity."

Echoing Vipin, Rahul says he sees Sushil "as my father" and consults him on every real estate deal the Kirloskars enter into. After the Ansal family partition, Rahul, like others in the family, noticed a perceptible change in Sushil's relationship with Pranav. "Pranav became a changed person after Uphaar and the partition crisis," Rahul says, "he became very protective of his father. We could see that change virtually overnight."

We made him an executive trainee," says Sushil, "and had him work in various departments – accounts, marketing, human resources, technical – for three months each. He was to eat with junior colleagues and did not have access to the lunch room used by senior executives and directors."

Actually, the family split had two implications for Sushil. He reshaped his business with a clear succession plan and a period of apprenticeship for Pranav. Secondly, he re-evaluated his dependence on his immediate family, and cultivated a more relaxed outlook to life that saw him invest even more in his role as a husband, father and grandfather. To understand the Sushil Ansal of 2010, both consequences deserve contemplation.

Pranav joined the business in 1990. It was an unusual debut for the son of a leading business family. "I made him independent from the first day," says Sushil, "gave him a loan of Rs 50,000 and asked him to execute a construction contract on his own." The contract was to build some houses in Gurgaon's Sushant Lok. It was the sort of training that Sushil's father had given him. Being thrown into the deep end, Pranav swam determinedly. In six months, he had surplus funds and was in a position to pay back his father. He made out a cheque and gave his first earnings to his mother. Kusum burst into tears.

The first test had been negotiated, but it was not going to be a smooth and lateral entry after that. Instead, from external contractor, Pranav was "promoted" to the lowest rung of the executive ladder in the Ansal API office. "We made him an executive trainee," says Sushil, "and had him work in various departments – accounts, marketing, human

SUSHIL AND KUSUM WITH ALPANA'S FAMILY
Alpana, Alika, Aman and Rahul

CLOSE KNIT

The tribulations of the past decade have given Kusum, Sushil and Pranav a unique bond

resources, technical – for three months each. He was to eat with junior colleagues and did not have access to the lunch room used by senior executives and directors."

There was a method to Sushil's regimen. "I had got thinking after reading Henry Ford's autobiography," he explains. "When his son came of age, Henry Ford sent him to the shop floor and made him tend to the machines. I wanted Pranav to know and appreciate every aspect and every task in the business."

Even after the training period was over, Pranav was not invited to join the API board. That was to happen only years later. In the interim, a small subsidiary, Ansal Townships and Projects, was set up for him and he was asked to execute projects in Rajasthan and Punjab. "He was the managing director and entirely on his own," says Sushil, "I was not even a director in Ansal Townships and Projects. I wanted him to learn the hard way, for that is the best way to learn."

A father-son and promoter-inheritor relationship in a business family is an inherently subtle one. Both men require their space and the father needs to understand when to step back. This is not always easy to understand, much less achieve. To his credit Sushil has been acutely conscious of it. "My father-in-law had four sons – Vinod, Pramod, Subodh and Ajit," he says, "all educated abroad, brilliant boys. Three returned. One stayed back in London. Their father was so overpowering and dominating a personality that I sometimes feel, without realising it, he perhaps didn't allow them enough space to blossom. Had they been on their own, with the freedom to think on their own, they would have fared much better... though all are doing well in life. The business he had established with such passion gradually died away due to several factors, mostly outside their control. I still feel sad about it."

Pranav looks at the dilemma from the other side. "If you're the son of a super-successful father," he says, candidly, "it's a double-edged sword. Expectations are pegged very high. Some people are happy living in the shadow of their fathers. Some look upon it as a platform to jump to the next level. I would like to believe I am in the second category." For Pranav, the family separation, which took place when he was in his late twenties, was an inflection point. "Before that my father and uncles were, frankly, overwhelming. They were just so hands-on in the business. The separation gave me an opportunity to prove myself and to come up quicker than would normally have happened. It was rather a blessing in disguise for me to shape a separate identity in the corporate world."

The late 1990s were a gruelling period, with the downturn, the separation and, of course, Uphaar. Does Pranav have any regrets? "Look at things this way," he says, "in the circumstances we did better than anybody expected us to. People had written us off. It took perseverance from my family, from my father and me and our colleagues, to get us where we are. Those were sub-normal conditions. You had to be mentally very strong to survive."

On a typical day, Sushil and Pranav meet only fleetingly but are available to each other when necessary. The father is the boss and has the right to exercise the veto but would clearly rather not. They are together at breakfast and dinner, if individual schedules permit, and try and meet at the office at some point between 12.30 and 2 p.m. "We go for meetings separately," says Pranav, "never together. It's a waste of resources. If one of us takes a call, the other will stand by it."

To Pranav, Sushil's reservoir of experience and insider knowledge of the real estate industry is an asset that needs to be tapped judiciously. "He keeps talking of retiring in five years," says the son of his father, "but to be honest it will be a gradual retirement. I want him to take it easy, though he will still spend six-seven hours looking at work-related matters. We are increasingly delegating decision-making to professionals. They will run the company, so that the promoters can do the strategic thinking. This is what will keep him busy."

Talking to Sushil and Pranav separately, it is interesting how alike they sound, almost completing each other's sentences. In a sense, this is suggestive of a shared temperament. Sheetal noticed this when she married into the Ansal family in 1993. "Both my father-in-law and my husband were never harrowed and hassled. The men in this family are like still waters. It's a gene passed on from father to son to, now, grandson."

"Both my father-in-law and my husband were never harrowed and hassled. The men in this family are like still waters. It's a gene passed on from father to son to, now, grandson".

A Bombay girl who by her own admission had lived a sheltered life and was a quiet student at Sydenham College, Sheetal found Delhi a dramatic change. To a large degree, her fears and anxieties were put at rest by the loving welcome she got from Pranav's family. Far from stuffy and stilted, the atmosphere in the busy household she was married into

THE CYCLE OF LIFE:
With his father's portrait looking on, Sushil passes on what he knows to his son.

THE MAGICAL DAY

Pranav at his wedding, flanked by his parents

was "fairly informal and easygoing." She is a favourite with her in-laws. Sushil says, "She has fine qualities of head and heart and is a pillar of the family, having strengthened bonds in tough times." For Kusum, Sheetal is not her daughter-in-law, but simply "my third daughter."

Sushil went out of his way to get to know Sheetal, a trait that is almost his trademark. "He is such a people person," says Sheetal, "and so very good at judging people. In a crowded room, he can strike up a conversation with a stranger, pick the best in him and make him feel special. It's a gift."

Sushil also had a zest for life that astonished Sheetal. One day she casually mentioned she was considering taking dancing lessons.

Before she knew it, Sushil had grabbed the idea. "Soon," says Sheetal, still incredulous, "the four of us, my in-laws, Pranav and me, were doing tango and salsa classes together." Later, Kusum, Sushil and Sheetal enrolled for an art appreciation course at the National Museum in Delhi. These were evening classes and he would attend after a full day at work. When Pranav and Sheetal were posted in Moscow in the early 1990s, while the Ansals were undertaking projects in Russia, Sushil would often come by and accompany Sheetal to the city's art galleries and museums. All this was a pleasant surprise for Sheetal: "At my parents' home, work was discussed at the dining table. Here mobiles are shut down and business calls are not taken. We have a drink and chat about everything from politics to cinema."

Her recollections highlight Sushil's typical attributes. First, he went out of his way to get to know and befriend his daughter-in-law and make her feel comfortable as the newest member of the family. This was important to him, and he made an effort towards it. He wanted to get to know her not merely on his terms but conscious of her individuality, her likes and dislikes. Secondly, by the early 1990s, with years of strenuous

A WARM WELCOME
Sushil and Kusum with the newly-married couple, Pranav and Sheetal, and Rajendra and Neelam Miglani (Sheetal's parents)

KUSUM AND SUSHIL WITH PRANAV'S FAMILY

Sheetal, Anushka, Pranav and Ayush

WE, THE FAMILY

Kusum and Sushil cherish moments when their children and grandchildren come together

work and the attainment of almost every career milestone behind him, he had begun to finally develop a sense of leisure. Always interested in art and travel, for instance, he began to prise open time for these pursuits.

Above
FOUR GENERATIONS
Sushil with his mother, and with Pranav and Pranav's then newborn son, Ayush

Facing page, top
BHAI DUJ
An intimate family occasion

Facing page, bottom left
GAME FOR IT
Sushil during a family holiday

Facing page, bottom right
EARLY START
Grandpa teaches Ayush golf

It hadn't always been like this. Archana says her first long family holiday with her father was not till she was fourteen. When it was time for school vacations, Sushil would send off his children with his brothers and their families, and stay back in Delhi to run the business. He would join Archana, Alpana and Pranav only for a weekend or a three-four day trip. Yet, his short presence would be marked by frenzy. As Alpana puts it, "He would make the most of the day – trekking, going outdoors, brisk walks in the hills, playing golf with us. Whenever he came, it woke up everybody."

To this day, her father's "energy and stamina" amazes Alpana. The Kirloskars and Ansals once went together to Egypt, to explore the pyramids and study the ancient culture. Sushil was clearly the livewire in

GRAND PRIX AF FRANKRIG
Juan Manuel Fangio
Karl Kling

the group. "Every evening we'd come back tired from sightseeing," Alpana says, "my husband, my mother-in-law, my mother would all retire. After a power nap, my father would be ready for more – the casino, a cultural show, whatever. He'd drag me out. He didn't want to waste a minute."

He is extremely fond of travelling, apart from enjoying ship and river cruises, and exploring the history and culture of different nations and civilisations. He could only satisfy his inner urge through adventures and exploring less frequented places. Archana remembers how he loved his trip with her brother Vinod, her sister-in-law Anju and friends Vijay and Mona to Latin America. She recalls "he visited Machu Picchu in Peru, stayed in a jungle lodge in Amazon forests amid wildlife, and had a motorboat ride in the rapids of the Iguaçu Falls in Brazil. Whether it's a trip to Masai Mara in Kenya or watching the dignified walk of the penguin in New Zealand or hunting a jungle fowl or fishing in the Amazon River, they are all a part of his life."

As family members stress, Sushil has this ability to compartmentalize and separate the personal from the professional; to ask his grandchildren about homework in the middle of a swirling day with the lawyers at the height of the Uphaar mess. Alpana illustrates this again with an example from her life. When in school, she had set her mind on becoming a doctor and was preparing for the medical entrance examinations. Playing a doting and concerned father, Sushil advised her against it. He told her that it would require years of education to qualify as a specialist in the medical field. Rather, he nudged her towards architecture, suggesting it was relevant to the family business.

Above
AT LEISURE
Holidaying with the grandchildren in Disneyland; hot air balloon safari certificate

Above

GAME FOR FUN

Despite his busy schedule, Sushil makes quality time for his grandchildren

Right

BLESSED MOMENTS

With Ayush and Anushka on his 70th birthday in Bangkok

THE GRANDCHILDREN

(Left to right) Aman, Alika, Abhishek, Anushka, Ayush and Sukriti

Persuaded, Alpana applied and got admission to the School of Planning and Architecture in Delhi. Graduating in 1987, she assisted the chief architect in a few Ansal projects before having one of her independent designs accepted for Palam Vihar. Soon she "branched into interiors" and offered "to do model homes for my father's company." Sushil jumped at the idea but, as Alpana discovered, could easily segregate a father's large heart from a businessman's clinical mind. "He handed me a ten-page contract," she laughs, "asked me to read it carefully, initial each page and sign it. And then he walked off, leaving me stunned!"

Each member of Sushil's immediate family has a unique relationship with him. These relationships has evolved and grown in the past decade, as the Ansals have rebuilt their lives after the setbacks of the late 1990s. Yet, the relationship that has grown and matured in the most beautiful manner is that between Sushil and the person who has shared the most with him, stood by him through every grimace and every smile and been his rock: his wife, Kusum.

If the break-up of the joint family hit Sushil hard, it was no less wounding for Kusum. This was a family she had nurtured at great cost

Above
BUILDING A HOME
Earth breaking at the site of Vishranti, with architect Satish Gujral

to herself and, in some cases, to their family unit. "When I came into the family," she says, "my brothers-in-law were very young. They were like kid brothers. My mother-in-law had had them late and was growing old. I brought up these boys, dressed and drove them to school. My youth was spent bringing up my brothers-in-law, finding girls for them, welcoming their brides into the house." Suddenly, all that remained were memories. "I loved them sincerely," Kusum continues, "but today I am reconciled to the fact that in relationships one should not expect anything in return. Only then can one remain happy and contented. I just performed my duty."

As Sushil took control of his life after Uphaar and the departure of his brothers, his equation with Kusum too started to evolve. They had had a lot of affection for, and respected each other, through the years. Now it was time to get to know each other, not out of a sense of duty or because of their relationship, but as two individuals in a marriage of equals. Fittingly, this fresh beginning coincided with a move into their dream house on 26 Feroze Shah Road, in the heart of Delhi, near the tall office towers of Connaught Place that had first put the Ansal brand on the map.

Above
SERENITY
Vishranti is an astonishingly quiet and calm building in the middle of Delhi's chaos

Inset
POWER OF PRAYER
At a family havan

ALL TOGETHER
The Ansal parivar

The house is a calm oasis in the midst of some of Delhi's busiest and most traffic-laden roads. Designed by the well-known architect, Satish Gujral, an old friend of the Ansal family, and built on a 1.5 acre plot that Sushil bought in 1996, it has high ceilings, large doors and windows, a parabolic roof, beautifully-carved marble floors, and high domes that merge with the architectural façade that Edwin Lutyens and Herbert Baker designed for the imperial city of Delhi. The house also has a private swimming pool and a small temple. It has an appropriate name: Vishranti, a combination of the Hindi/Sanskrit words for rest and peace. Perhaps Gujral realised what Kusum and Sushil craved was tranquillity and a private refuge. This is what awaited them as they moved in, in November 2001. Sushil and Kusum echo "we are thankful to Satish Gujral and his son Mohit, his daughter Raseel and her husband Naveen, for designing the house inside and outside, creating an ambience which we wanted. We are enjoying living here."

The house and its sensibility are emblematic of where Kusum and Sushil are today, their labour done, their duties performed, their children settled, their debts paid. It represents the common space they have created. Yet, the serenity had to be earned and worked towards, and took years of struggle.

Kusum is different from the archetypal Delhi business wife of her generation in that she has never been willing to sit back and merely enjoy her husband's wealth, but has sought to carve out her own niche. A writer and a poet – she did her PhD midway through her marriage,

Facing page
IN HER OWN RIGHT
While being the perfect corporate wife, Kusum never lost sight of her own identity as a writer

Above left
EXTENDED FAMILY
Kusum and Sushil with Kusum's brothers and sisters-in-law

Above right
FAMILY FUN
Sushil and Kusum dancing with Surendra Kumar and Asha Rani (Kusum's parents)

while bringing up three children and supervising a large and perpetually packed household – Kusum wrote a deeply moving and searingly honest memoir in the mid-1990s. Published in English under the title *As I Am* (1997), the book talks of Kusum's early years, the loss of her mother, being brought up by an uncle and aunt, the fears of her father who was keen to marry her off and who perhaps came in the way of an academic career. Kusum's father had been impressed enough in his one meeting with Sushil to see him as the right match. Vinod Saigal, the oldest of Kusum's siblings and today a close friend and colleague of Sushil's, recalls that initial impression: "I've found a boy, my father told us, with a spirit of enterprise and the will to make a mark. He'd seen that drive towards achievement."

Nevertheless Kusum's marital home held its challenges. "I came from an almost all-male home. There was no mother, elder sister or sister-in-law to advise me. I had no one to counsel me on how to settle into an in-laws' family, no one to offer tips." The result was a cultural shock. Sushil's parents were conservative and this called for compromises on Kusum's part, compromises that were not always easy or willingly made. "Mine was a different background," she says, "my grandfather was a barrister who had studied in England, my grandmother was a graduate in an era when very few Indian women were educated. At our home in Aligarh, art and culture was part of the mix, *mushairas* and musical concerts were regular features, poets dropped in very often."

The Ansals were a world apart. They lived low-key lives and were not regulars at cultural events or even avid readers. It was Kusum who introduced these habits; this was her "charter" she says. There was resistance to at least some of her notions. In *As I Am*, she recounts how her mother-in-law did not take kindly to visits by some of her literary friends from Aligarh, one of whom was Muslim. Kusum, however, stood her ground and gradually, over years, conquered old mindsets.

What united Kusum and Sushil in those initial days was a sense of duty. Kusum pushed aside her literary aspirations for the family; Sushil single-mindedly built the family business and refused to take on his parents even when he knew they were wrong, such as in the case of Kusum's friend from Aligarh. However, he was amazingly supportive when Kusum decided to finally seek a literary career and take part in theatre, accompanying her to the offices of publishers in

AS WINTER SETS IN:
A relaxed evening with the Ansals

अजनबी धुँआ

वहाँ पथरीली चारदीवारी में
अपनी मुलाकातों के दौरान
पता नहीं क्यों तुम्हें देख नहीं पाती
तुम्हारी आँखों के गुबार की वजह से
उठता हुआ अजनबी धुँआ...
मेरी रूह के चारों तरफ लिपट जाता है।

अखबार के पर्चों से जो गर्द उमड़ती है
कहाँ बयाँ कर पाती है हमारी उदासी
हमारे बेकसूर हाल की असली दास्ताँ..
पर लोगों की फुसफुसाहट से घुमड़ता कड़वापन
मेरी रूह के चारों तरफ लिपट जाता है।

मैं उस कमरे की घुटीली हवा में
भरपूर कोशिश करती हूँ.. कि
मेरी आँखों की मुहब्बत
उस सन्नाटे को शब्द दे दे
और मैं सुन लूँ वह जो तुम कह नहीं पाते..
एक रहस्य जो तुम्हारी रूह से उठ मेरे मन में लिपटता है..
मत चिंता करो मेरे प्रिय..
आत्मा का सच.. सच होता है
और वही इन खबरों में कहानियों का लिखा जाकर
मुक्त करेगा हमारी रूह को.. इंसाफ दिलाकर,
झूठी बदनामियों की स्याही से।

कुसुम अंसल

विश्रान्ति, एन-148, पंचशील पार्क, नई दिल्ली-110 017
फोन : 6438388, 6433618 फैक्स : 011-3322009

Daryaganj and managing the house as she left for Bombay for an extended period when one of her novels, *Ek aur Panchvati*, was made into a feature film by the famous director Basu Bhattacharya. Produced by Shobha Doctor, the film starred Akbar Khan, Suresh Oberoi and Deepti Naval. It was screened in several film festivals and won three international awards.

In her book, Kusum lays bare experiences others would have preferred to cover up. On one occasion, she went with her contribution to the editor of a Hindi journal, the office of which neighboured Ansal Bhawan. He was openly condescending, but Kusum was undeterred. It speaks of Kusum's perseverance that she refused to rest on her husband's identity. It speaks of Sushil's sensitivity that he understood this was important to her and backed her as best he could. It is this mutual respect that has underpinned their partnership. Despite the ups and downs and occasional differences of opinion, it has allowed them to raise amazingly "normal" and down-to-earth children. It has given them – and their family – the resilience to survive, recover and flower after the tribulations at the turn of the millennium. "She stood by me like a rock and gave me strength and courage and showed great perseverance during my journey in a life full of ups and downs," says Sushil.

That is why, well after his companies' balance sheets are assessed and his buildings tabulated for carpet area, Sushil Ansal must be measured against the ultimate yardstick: his success as a family man.

AT ONE WITH NATURE
Kusum and Sushil have a remarkably green home

ALONE, TOGETHER

Kusum Ansal on her husband – and their life

Friendship is an investment of time and money. In the course of his endeavour to build a business in the hitherto unknown field of real-estate development, Sushil had very little time, nor enough money, to invest in friendships. Whatever time he had, he invested in raising his school-going brothers and unmarried sisters.

I walked with him, hand in hand, to maintain the equilibrium of emotions and professional commitments, and to keep the family together as a unit. There was little time for holidays, parties, birthday celebrations. Even Sundays were generally working days. Life was so full of unavoidable obstacles that Sushil overlooked his children. He was so caught up with his work that he could not attend my brother Pramod's wedding in Aligarh.

Years passed. The sisters got married, business stabilized. Sushil began to make friends at the Rotary Club of Delhi (South), becoming its president in 1978. Meetings were held at the Hotel Intercontinental. He was a respected figure and people cited him for his principles, generosity and compassion. He made friends like Amrit Sarna, Chaman Sahni, Vijay Aggarwal, Shyam Sahni, Balraj Sondhi and Chote Bharani. They spent quality time travelling together.

In particular, Amrit and Chaman Sahni were very close to Sushil. Chaman renounced the materialism of this world and took sanyas in 2002, leaving his prosperous business and family. It is unheard of in these times and was quite an emotional blow to Sushil, who looked upon him as a sounding board. For his part, Amrit is an elder brother to Sushil. He has been quite unwell for the past ten years and has stopped leaving the house. This has created a vacuum in Sushil's life as the families are very close. As Samuel Peterson said, "Friends are needed both for joy and for sorrow."

Loneliness could never interrupt Sushil's capacity for work. He perhaps fills this emotional void by making his work both a pilgrimage and passion. He possesses boundless energy, a healthy impatience and

yearning desire. He leaps out of his office chair to bring home ideas and thoughts that add to his company's prospects. Without this zest, the colonies of Sushant Lok and Palam Vihar would not have come up, the adventures in Iraq and Thailand would not have happened.

Sadly, when it was time to enjoy the fruits of a life well spent in hard work, the Uphaar tragedy took place. It was a revealing moment. As the poet Tuslidas wrote in *Ramcharitmanas*:

Dhiraj, dharma, mitra aur naree
Aapad kaal, parakhiye charee

One's own patience, conduct, friends and life partner
are tested during adversity

To me, the Uphaar episode revealed two stunning truths. First, the media has become so powerful in our society, especially after several TV channels started 24/7 telecasting. It at times pronounces judgement even without a full investigation or knowledge of all aspects of a case. Instead of placing the unbiased facts before the public and letting it arrive at its own conclusions, the media had decided against the Ansals from the first moment. Hysteria is sometimes created by unlimited freedom

Facing page, top
TALKING SHOP
Discussing business with Willy, a hotelier associate from Switzerland, and old friend and management guru, Ashok Kapur

Facing page, bottom
SUSHIL'S FARM PARTY
(L-R)Sham, Amrit, Chaman and Satt with their spouses

Above
CHAMPAGNE TIME AT A NEW YEAR'S EVE PARTY
With friends (left to right) Vijay, Shivraj, and Kewal

Inset
OLD MATE
Sushil and his friend Chaman

Facing page
CONTEMPLATIVE MOOD:
Friends say for a hard-nosed businessman, Sushil is remarkably emotional

Below
EYE TO THE NEIGHBOUR
Seeing China from Nathu La, above Leh

Bottom
AT IGUAÇU FALLS, BRAZIL
Sushil loves travel and exploration

of expression. I wonder if this sometimes tends to influence judges...? In the eyes of the law, there should be no difference between government officials and those in the private sector. All are equal. In reality, it does not happen so. In the Uphaar case, senior government officials were not charged. When it came to the private sector, even former directors, who had nothing to do with day-to-day operations, were not spared. Why? That question remains unanswered.

Second, the attitude of Sushil's brothers, Gopal and Deepak, and their families came as a shock. Even today, fourteen years on, Sushil and I cannot fully comprehend their betrayal. Perhaps it is too personal a matter for me to write about here, but it is a reality that, I fear, will stay, with Sushil and me for the rest of our lives. The wound is still nurtured in my heart and is bleeding.

*****

Today, past 70, Sushil deserves a peaceful life. Having worked hard to taste business success, he misses the satisfaction of quiet and tranquillity. It is the divine rhythm of prayer within his heart that keeps him going. He is at his calmest, I suspect, when in prayer, when deep in the ritual of a havan in our little temple at home, or when giving back to society in the form of one of his many philanthropic missions.

IN AUGUST COMPANY

Kusum and Sushil with Indira Gandhi, former Prime Minister of India

With Giani Zail Singh, former President of India

With K.R. Narayanan, former President of India

With Bill Clinton, former American president

With I.K. Gujral, former Prime Minister of India

With Atal Bihari Vajpayee, former Prime Minister of India

With L. K. Advani, former Home Minister of India

With Pranab Kumar Mukherjee, India's current Finance Minister

With Arjun Singh, former Human Resource Development minister

With Yashwant Sinha, former Finance Minister

With Salman Khurshid, the present Corporate Affairs Minister

With the Honorable Gordon Campbell: Premier of Canada 11/11/03

Diplomatic hand: With Hiroshi Hirabayashi, former Japanese ambassador to India, at an embassy function

With Mr. Somprasong Ajchaiyava (extreme left), the Thai partner in the Bangkok project

With Montek Singh Ahluwalia, college mate and now Deputy Chairman of the Planning Commission

With Bimal Jalan, former Reserve Bank Governor

With scholar-politician Karan Singh

With Atal Behari Vajpayee and R.K. Dhawan at Pranav's wedding

With Mr L K Advani, former Home Minister of India

Warrior hero: With Field Marshal Sam Manekshaw

With the late Sunil Dutt, politician and movie star,

With Satish Modi and Preston Bush (brother of US President, George Bush)

FICCI delegation in Kathmandu

Leading a business mission to Canada: Sushil and other mission members are seen here with Divyabh Manchanda, India's Consul General in Toronto at the time

PHASE SIX

CITIZEN ANSAL

Sushil has always been conscious of the larger social responsibility that comes with success and wealth. For him, corporate social responsibility is not a cliché and a trigger for a press release, but something instinctive, flowing from the deepest recesses of his being. Much of his charitable or philanthropic work is embedded in a framework and sensibility that makes sense to him as an Indian, and serves a utilitarian purpose in the society he knows best. An astute businessman to his bones, rather than just doling out donations at random, he prefers to create sustainable charitable or social welfare institutions that would run professionally.

Historically, Sushil argues, in the archetypal Indian village, the temple was not just a place of worship but the principal public space for discussions, panchayat meetings, families to meet in the evenings and cultural events. It strikes Sushil as remarkable that the more India changes, the more it remains the same. "The draw and appeal of religion remain very strong," he says, "in fact the younger generation is more religious today than their parents or grandparents may have been. I have seen it in my family." Kusum's influence has been marked here. She comes from an Arya Samaji family – her grandmother was among the founders of the Arya Samaj in Aligarh – and, every morning, prays and performs Vedic rituals in the small temple at home. In Delhi, Sushil has long pondered the astonishing popularity of the Akshardham temple. In the five years since it has opened, the temple complex has already become one of the city's leading tourist attractions and civic monuments. There is a message here that Sushil cannot ignore.

As a person, Sushil does not believe in idol worship or visiting temples frequently. Nevertheless he is a god-fearing man and feels the divine lives in one's soul and heart. Human service, his parents taught him, is the best form of worship. Despite this, he has observed how

Left

WITH THE DIVINE

Greeting the Shankaracharya of Kanchi

Below

HOSTING HOLINESS

Swami Dayanandji and Swami Prabhudnandanji come home for lunch

Left

SEEKING BLESSINGS

At Ajmer Sharif

Below

AMONG HIS OWN

At a gurudwara in his ancestral village of Khamma, Jalandar

people's faith in god and religion has helped them get inner peace and solace. In today's strife-torn world, with its physical and psychological tensions, people tend to be drawn to temples for relief and calm. Sushil therefore believes in creating places of worship where one can experience peace and tranquillity. Sushil's first such experience was when Ashok Varma, his sister Meenakshi's husband, introduced him to Baba Nagpalji, founder of the famous Chattarpur Temple complex in south Delhi. Sushil met Baba Nagpalji in the early 1990s when Babaji was sitting with a blueprint of the proposed expansion of the Mata Ka Mandir, part of his temple complex. He blessed Sushil and said, "You have to build this part of the temple for us." Sushil recalls that meeting: "I couldn't turn him down. It was a command as well as a blessing. Babaji's penetrating eyes mesmerised me." Today, the extended portion of the temple is visited by tens of thousands of devotees every month.

Another indication of Sushil's consciousness of people's faith in religion is the building of the International Society for Krishna Consciousness (ISKON) Centre called the Ansal API ISKON Centre in Sushant Golf City in Lucknow. The association between the Sushil's

FUTURE PLANS
With the international head of the Swaminarayan sect, parent organisation of the Akshardham temples. Megapolis will see an Akshardham temple

family and ISKON is an old one. In the 1970s, Surendra Kumar Saigal, Kusum's father and an ISKCON follower, had introduced Sushil to Swami Prabhupadaji, the founder of the Krishna Consciousness movement. Sushil and Kusum had been very impressed by the Swami's erudition and a relationship was born. In Lucknow, Ansal API has given ISKCON five acres of land, worth Rs 15 crore at current rates, at no charge, where a massive temple complex is being built. The design will incorporate a museum devoted to the "religious ethos of India," an auditorium for religious discourses and appropriate cultural events and rooms for visitors to stay in. Sushil would like to thank Gopal Krishna Goswamy, Governing Body commissioner of ISKCON, Srestha Das, Devakinandan Das and the Board of Governors of ISKCON's Lucknow unit for giving him an opportunity to contribute to this spiritual centre.

The construction of the Ansal API ISKON Centre is estimated to cost Rs 60 crore. Money will come from voluntary donations – buyers of property in Sushant Golf City can choose to contribute if they so wish – and will be topped up by the Ansal family. Sushil hopes this complex will eventually come to be recognised as a "philosophical and spiritual

OLD ASSOCIATION

Being felicitated at an ISCKON function in Lucknow

centre" and that its *gurukul* and Vedanta institute will go a long way in preserving India's ancient heritage. Smaller centres in collaboration with ISKCON are planned for the Ansal townships in Jaipur (three acres) and Jodhpur (two acres). As usual, he has set the bar high.

Facing Page
NEW START
Earth breaking ceremony of API ISKCON centre at Sushant Golf City, Lucknow

Below
CHATTARPUR TEMPLE, NEW DELHI
The Ansals built a part of the complex

Kusum, an ardent student of Vedanta literature, has studied the Vedas and the Gita in depth under the guardianship of the very learned and respected Swami Prabudanandji, the founder of Arsh Vidya Mandhir and a disciple of Swami Dayanandji. Swami Dayanandji founded the Shri Ganga Dhreswar Trust which runs several centres all over the world, teaching about the great epics of India and spiritualism. Sushil attends only a few of their courses due to limited time "but I try to retain and practice the philosophies in daily life and find them extremely beneficial," he says. Whenever Swami Dayanandji stays at his home, "I utilise his presence and blessings by asking all my inquisitive and never-ending questions to try to understand the unknown and attain internal peace and tranquillity," says Sushil.

Sushil owns a room in their ashram on the banks of the river in Rishikesh, and once in a while Kusum and Sushil escape from their tough daily routine to relax and absorb the soothing vibrations, following the ashram rules, routine and food. "Every stay at the ashram is an unforgettable and rejuvenating experience," avers Sushil.

Swami Dayanandji has started AIM for Seva, an all India movement based on the principle of caring for the marginalised sections of society, particularly the tribals and other communities cut off from mainstream society. Swamiji has nominated Sushil as his Treasurer and Dr. M.P. Narayanan as President. The programme provides free

GURU OF JOY
With Shri Shri Ravi Shankar

education, health, training and vocational programmes and social and economic integration for the remote tribals into the mainstream. Today it has benefited thousands of people all over the country. Sushil wishes he could devote more time to this laudable cause.

Sushil is highly impressed by the practical preaching of Shri Shri Ravi Shankarji and the Art of Living course which is a great destressing medium in the modern life. He was quite mesmerized during a personal chat with Shri Shri Ravi Shankar when he blessed his home in Feroze Shah Road and opened his heart to him on various international, national and personal issues. Swamiji's vast in-depth knowledge kept Sushil amazed and since then he snatches every opportunity to seek his advice and wisdom.

Sushil first visited Delhi's famous Akshardam temple complex when he was invited to celebrate the birthday of one of the Hinduja brothers. Going around the complex Sushil was impressed not only by the architectural beauty and rich carvings, but by Shri Swami Narayan sect's deep-rooted philosophy of spiritualism. Bochasanwasi Shri Aksharpurushottam Swaminarayan Sanstha is an international socio-spiritual NGO, affiliated with the United Nations, selflessly serving peoples of all races, cultures and religions. The Sanstha has over 9,000 centres throughout the world, and over 550,000 volunteers for more than 160 humanitarian activities. The sanstha is headed by

Param Pujya Pramukh Swami Maharaj, who inspired the Akshardham Temple in Gujarat and Delhi. In July 2010, Sushil had a meeting with J. Swaminarayan Ramachandra Barotji, Sadhu Atma Swarup Dasji and Sadhu Premdasji where he offered three acres of land to the Akshardham temple management to build a complex in Megapolis, a new city the Ansals are building adjoining Greater Noida (*see chapter* 7). It is proposed as a spiritual and cultural complex, which will impart moral values to the children, youth and adults of all sections of society irrespective of their caste, social and financial status. The complex will consist of a temple and assembly hall, an exhibition of Indian heritage, a de-addiction centre, a Bal Sanskar Kendra, Kishore Sanskar Kendra, Mahila Kendra, cultural gardens, a dormitory for swamis and a dormitory for volunteers. Sushil is also helping to complete an Ayyappa temple in Noida. Since Kusum is an Arya Samaji, the Ansal family's contribution and commitment to various Arya Samaj complexes is a continuing process.

Humans need spiritualism to nourish their souls, but also need wisdom for their minds. While working for the Human Welfare Mission founded by his father, Sushil used to supervise the running of schools in slum areas. He helped distribute free books, slates and pencils to poor children. This created a lifelong relationship with education. The ultimate in social infrastructure, as Sushil sees it, is the provision of quality educational institutions. "If you are assured of a good school in a neighbourhood, one your child will be happy in, it will make it easier for you to consider buying or renting a house or an apartment."

In this regard, the challenge before Sushil is enormous: Lucknow's Sushant Golf City and Megapolis alone will need over 200 schools. Obviously, the Ansals can't build and run all the schools. Land is being offered to a variety of leading schools to set up campuses and branches in the new cities. Yet, with education being a family obsession since the days of Chiranji Lal, it is also being spun off as a separate division. Headquartered in Dubai, GEMS Education, flagship of the well-known businessman Sunny Varkey, is among the world's largest education service providers. It has entered into an agreement with Ansal API to build and operate schools in the two cities. Typically, the Ansals provide the land and the building – constructed to GEMS specifications – and the Varkey-led team actually runs the school. GEMS International

School has started in Palam Vihar, with a capacity of 2,000 children.

An agreement has also been entered into with Educomp Solution, India's largest education company, to set up Millennium Schools, an Educomp brand, in various townships being developed by Ansal API. Already Educomp has started operating schools in Ansal townships in Kurukshetra, Panipat and Meerut. Land at subsidised rates has also been given to G.D. Goenka School in Lucknow, Springdales School in Jaipur and Delhi Public School in Sushant Lok, Gurgaon. The idea is to draw good metropolitan institutions to Tier I and Tier II cities, where there is need for quality education facilities.

Schools are not new to Sushil's life. His involvement in the field of education follows two parallel courses. The business arm is Knowledge Tree Infrastructure. Supplementing and preceding this is the Chiranjiv Charitable Trust that has, for several years now, run and supported the

LEARNING CURVE
Chiranjiv Bharti, a tribute to Sushil's father, is one of the many schools initiated by the Chiranjiv Bharti Trust

Gyan Bharati School in south Delhi and the Chiranjiv Bharati School in Gurgaon's Sushant Lok and Palam Vihar. Founded and sustained as part of the Ansals' CSR initiatives, they are recognised as among the leading schools in their respective cities. Chiranjiv Bharati is, in fact, now an Ansal chain, with branches in Gurgaon, Ghaziabad and Lucknow. Students are subsidised on a merit-cum-means basis to enable them to pursue their studies and serve the country when they grow up.

In her autobiography, Kusum describes the early days at Gyan Bharati. The founder-chairman of the school trust was the well-known scholar and parliamentarian, L.M. Singhvi. Other trustees included such eminent people as O.P. Jain, doyen of the arts and crafts world, Sudharshan Aggarwal, later to become governor of Uttarakhand and Sikkim, and O.P. Vaish, who heralded the polio eradication programme in India through Rotary International. These were the people who had asked Sushil and his father to set up a school in Delhi on seven acres of land allotted by the DDA in the Saket area. Sushil needed a good principal to start Gyan Bharati School. He approached M.M. Kapoor, principal of Modern School, where his three children had studied. Kapoor was about to retire and agreed to join Gyan Bharati. It was the best start the school could get. Kusum was very involved with the school for several years and went there regularly, especially after Mr. Kapoor retired.

If Kusum was the backbone of the education philanthropy mission, it is only fitting that Sheetal is assisting Sushil in the education business venture. She manages Knowledge Tree Infrastructure. In 2009, Sheetal and Pranav travelled to Singapore to tie up with Mind Champs, an internationally-known name in the field of play schools. David Chiem and Teo Wee Jone of Mind Champs visited India and identified a few sites. The first Mind Champs School in India can be expected to open in 2011. This venture is taking place under the rubric of Knowledge Tree Infrastructure. Around 20,000 children will study in these schools in the next five years.

Sushil is certain and emphatic that the twenty-first-century schools the family will nurture will be different in sensibility and approach from traditional institutions. "With Mr Varkey, Educomp and Mind Champs," he says, "we have chosen partners who focus on creative, lateral modes of imparting education. Not mugging up." Pranav puts it bluntly: "We need to make an impact in education. Yes, there

is a commercial aspect to it, but it is also an attempt to plough back to society. I was at Modern School and thirty years later sent my children there. I found they were studying the same things, the same books, the same examples. I pulled them out. It got me thinking. Globally, even the IB [International Baccalaureate] system is being thought of as outmoded. Here we are still discussing CBSE [Central Board of Secondary Education] reform… This has to change."

Sushil is a wide-spectrum man and his interest and purpose in primary and school education has only been matched by his meticulous planning for the family's projects in higher education. The Chiranjiv Charitable Trust has been running the Ansal Institute of Technology (AIT) for the past decade and the Sushant School of Art and Architecture (SSAA) for the past two decades. Located in Gurgaon, adjacent to each other, the two will soon function under the umbrella of a university, clearance for which is at an advanced stage.

While seemingly a small part of Sushil's professional life, the story of the setting up of the SSAA, and later the AIT, merits recounting. If nothing else, it establishes his singular ability to attract and work with gifted, out-of-the-ordinary individuals. In the best traditions of a skilful human resource manager, Sushil is flexible enough to mould his organization to suit the demands and sometimes idiosyncrasies of talented people who may not otherwise be able or willing to conform to an assembly-line process.

Set up on a makeshift campus on the Mehruali-Gurgaon Road in 1989, the SSAA moved to its present home – Sector 55, Gurgaon – in 1997. By then, its reputation had already been built, thanks primarily to its founder dean (now dean emeritus) Man Singh M. Rana, among India's most formidable post-Independence architects. Getting Rana to agree to steer a start-up architecture school was a coup. The man had seriously

MEMORIES TO TREASURE
A convocation ceremony at SSAA with the late Madhavrao Scindia as the chief guest

impressive credentials. An alumnus of the Sir J.J. College of Architecture in Bombay, Rana apprenticed under Frank Lloyd Wright in the United States, before being drawn back to India by Jawaharlal Nehru.

In India, Rana undertook a series of teaching and design assignments, including conceptualising freedom fighter Asaf Ali's tomb and, later, Delhi's Buddha Jayanthi Park, to commemorate the 2500th birth anniversary of Gautam Buddha. In this period, he served as the chief architect of the New Delhi Municipal Council (NDMC). Sushil met him because his approval was required for buildings they were planning to construct in the NDMC area. It was about twenty years after this early interaction that Sushil sought out and, in his trademark manner, diligently and politely pursued Rana. The moment was ripe for a cutting-edge architecture school, one that would combine traditional Indian aesthetics and modes of urban planning with the needs of a modern cityscape. Rana was his first and only choice for the dean's job.

"We started off with 40 students," recalls Rana, who still takes classes, "and now have 80 in every batch." The five-year undergraduate course at SSAA is much sought after. Graduates of the SSAA can be found all over the world. It has exchange programmes with six well-known international architecture institutions – from the University of Melbourne, Australia, to the Aristotle University, Thessaloniki, Greece, to the Frank Lloyd Foundation, in the United States. Rana envisioned the SSAA not as a plain architect factory but as a workshop for moulding aesthetic sensibilities. Sushil backed him all the way. Between them Rana, Sushil and Kusum used their resources and network to draw the finest minds to the SSAA. The artist M.F. Husain was a frequent visitor and inspired the young minds he interacted with.

Looking back at the institution he built, Rana has only two complaints. First, he says, Sushil doesn't find the time to visit as often

LEARNING ALL THE TIME
With students of SSAA

BORED GAME

COMMONWEALTH GAMES HOUSING

NURTURING CREATIVITY

Sushant School of Art and Architecture

as he used to, "though Mrs Ansal comes here more often." Second, in all these years "we have never been given Ansal's projects." The second complaint is actually a compliment. Sushil never intended the SSAA as a cheap and ready source of designs for his business ventures. He kept the two enterprises separate. As a man who helped shape metropolitan cities and who was passionate about urban spaces, he saw the architecture school as an effort to contribute to society.

Sushil is grateful to J.R. Bhalla, an institution in himself in the field of architecture and former president of the Architecture Council of India, for accepting the post of first chairman of the Governing Body of the SSAA. Bhalla and Rana got emotionally involved in growing the institution. They were assisted by Chander Kukreja of Kukreja and Associates, as well as several other eminent architects. After Bhalla's retirement, Sushil chairs the Governing Body. The SSAA today is one of the top three architectural institutes in the Asian subcontinent, according to the EUMD India list of top architectural institutions by the British Council. Pranav and Sushil have inducted Manit Rastogi, a young and dynamic visionary architect, into the Governing Body to help it set even higher benchmarks. "Sushant School is taking a leadership role by responding to the growing need for multifaceted professionals with the grounding in traditional design, theory and practice to meet the future needs of a rapidly developing Indian economy and society and the challenges of sustainable development," says Rastogi. Michael Knowles, Dean of Sushant School of Design says "Design is the art of every great

civilisation. We try to ignite in our students, creativity, functionality and aesthetic comfort which if harnessed can enhance the quality of life."

The mandate of the AIT, next door to the SSAA, was no different when it was set up in 2000. In January that year, the building was being completed and Sushil was a worried man. He was still looking for a director. There was no dearth of applicants but he wanted somebody who would give the AIT a different character.

At this point M.P. Singh, a professor of engineering at the Indian Institute of Technology in Delhi till the 1990s but having subsequently moved to a university in the United States, came to see Sushil. He was in India on vacation and had heard about the upcoming AIT. He sought a meeting with the Ansal API team and suggested the AIT's engineering students be given the facility of completing part of their education in a partner university in the United States. Sushil jumped at the idea. "He didn't want a traditional institution," explains Singh, "he wanted one that was in training mode from day one."

The deal was done but Sushil had one condition. He wanted Singh to run the institution. Singh was initially reluctant but Sushil, unfailingly polite, nevertheless refused to take no for an answer. "For nine months I worked in an honorary capacity," says Singh, "finally I gave in and became the director."

The AIT began by offering degree courses for a Bachelor in Business Administration (BBA) and a Bachelor in Computer Applications (BCA). For three years the students studied in India. In their final

STRIVING FOR EXCELLENCE
Students at the Ansal Institute of Technology

year, they went to a university in the United States, had their credits transferred and eventually got degrees from the affiliated US university. The AIT started with 90 students; ten years later it has 2,000. The foreign affiliation began with South Carolina University but today extends to a dozen universities in the United States, Canada, Australia and New Zealand. Students invariably go overseas on scholarships, provided they attain a minimum Grade Point Average (GPA), and their parents don't face a pressing financial burden. Each year 300 or 400 students from the AIT get to go abroad as part of such "twin" programmes. "We aim to increase this to 1,000 students," says Sushil.

In 2008, the AIT began a four-year Bachelor in Technology programme in disciplines such as computer engineering and mechanical

engineering. It also offers courses in emergent fields such as biotechnology and nanotechnology. Walking down the expansive, fifteen-acre campus of the AIT, it is difficult not to be impressed by the scale and attention to detail, right down to the hostel where students live. Like always, Sushil and his team have left nothing to chance.

Yet, Sushil seldom comes to the AIT campus, though as chairman of the Governing Body he is always available for help. Singh describes his equation with his boss: "He trusts people, never interferes. In all these years, he has never asked me for an out-of-turn admission or favour." There was only one exception to this otherwise spotless record. "It was a case involving one of Mr Ansal's drivers," Singh says, "a person who had been serving him for decades. He wanted a special fee concession

EDUCATION CAMPUS
Ansal Institute of Technology

for the driver's child. It was the first time that he requested a financial concession that was not in conformity with the fee system."

AIT campuses are planned for Sushant Golf City (Lucknow) and Megapolis (Dadri). "Once we have university status," says Sushil, "we are also hoping to open campuses abroad and have identified Thailand and Dubai as locations with potential." The thrust, he says, is for an education system that has linkages with industry and with the demands of the emerging economy. For instance, the AIT is starting a postgraduate diploma programme for those aiming to work in real-estate and property development companies. This offers a complete orientation of the business and readies the candidate for multiple roles – usually beginning as a management trainee – in Ansal API or peer companies. A similar programme for retail sector professionals – deemed necessary given the organised retail boom in India – has also been inaugurated.

Whether it is schools or colleges and universities, Sushil emphasises he is concerned with "excellence, not numbers." Even so, numbers do tell a tale. The component institutions of what will eventually become a university have about 3,000 students between them. "In four years," says Sushil, "I would want this figure to go up to 10,000." Schools owned or partnered by Ansal group charities or companies cover a total of 15,000 pupils today. In three years this should expand to double the size.

BRAIN AND BRAWN
Inauguration of the Sports Complex at AIT

Not all of this growth will be driven by giveaways and endowments. To Sushil's mind, the best form of philanthropy is that which creates sustainable entities and projects and institutionalises a symbiotic relationship with the Ansal business empire. This entails making effective use of Ansal API's skills and resources for the betterment of society, so that both the company and the external community have a stake in each other. As a philosophy it is not very different from the logic Google offered while announcing its social sector arm, Google.org.

The best exposition of this vision is the Education Cities that will be integral to both Megapolis and Sushant Golf City. One hundred and fifty acres of land in the Lucknow project and fifty acres in Dadri have been set aside for these Education Cities. Ansal API will be responsible for the infrastructure and will develop common libraries, sports facilities, auditoria and hostels. Then, it will lease or sell plots of around 20 acres to different universities and education service providers.

"The higher education sector is being opened by the government," says Sushil, "and there are enough foreign technical and vocational training institutions that want to come. They would appreciate a readymade campus, and not want to begin from scratch." The presence of such an ambitious education hub will also add intellectual capital and investor value to the new cities and enrich their social infrastructure. Facilities in the Education City can be customised for a client or partner university and plot sizes can be expanded as required. "This is actually a Chinese model," Sushil says, "that Pranav picked up while travelling. We have adapted it to Indian conditions."

At the other end of the chain, in the vicinity of both Megapolis and Sushant Golf City, the Ansals are adopting village schools, as well as upgrading dispensaries and providing for doctor visits. "The villages that we adopt are provided with all weather roads, street lights, potable drinking water, sewers, waste disposal system, upgraded schools and improved hygiene," says Sushil. Overall, thirty villages have been linked to the Ansal group. "This is CSR plus business," Sushil says, rather frankly, "the jobs and market demands of the new cities we are building will require educated young people. It makes sense for local village youth to become eligible for the jobs in Megapolis or in Sushant Golf City, rather than lose out to migrants from faraway districts. We have to give the local community a stake in development."

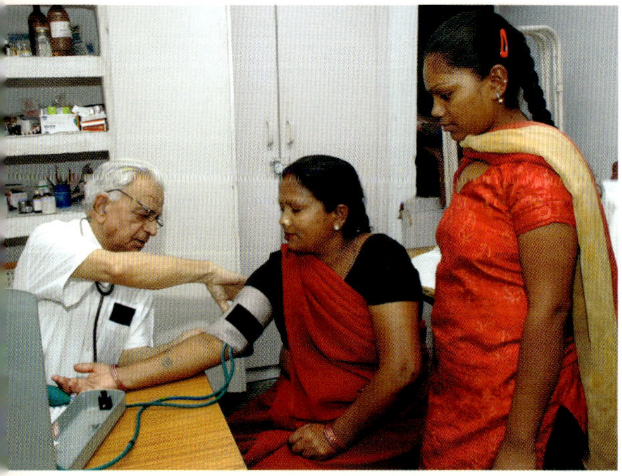

SOCIAL SERVICE:
Shanti Sahyog, catering to the poorer sections of Delhi, has been an Ansal-supported project for years

From the Rotary Club to Kiwanis International, Sushil has been associated with a number of social-service organisations. In particular, Kiwanis is close to his heart. In India, the social service organisation was started by Dharam Vira, a doyen of the Indian Civil Service and later governor of West Bengal, and industrialists Bharat Ram and Charat Ram as well as leading citizens such as Air Chief Marshal O.P. Mehra, General O.P. Malhotra, Satti Punj, O.P. Khaitan and Ajit Sud and others. Sushil, being a member of the Board of Governors, helped construct the over 80,000-square-foot Kiwanis Centre in Delhi's Qutab Institutional Area. Here, over 1,000 artificial limbs are provided annually to those who need them, at highly subsidised rates.

The Kiwanis mission leaves Sushil emotionally satisfied. Philanthropy, as he never ceases to remind you, is an inheritance from his father and Chiranji Lal's Human Welfare Mission. In 1976, the Mission was incorporated into the Chiranjiv Charitable Trust and now it is poised for another metamorphosis – to the Sushil Ansal Foundation.

As a student, Sushil helped his father run dispensaries in slum colonies. The issue of equitable access to health care has always exercised him. As the years passed, he sponsored a homoeopathic dispensary in Ansal Bhawan, in the heart of Delhi. Later, two other charitable medical centres, in south Delhi and in Palam Vihar, Gurgaon, were opened. In the slums of Kalkaji, an NGO called Shanti Sahyog runs a health centre that is a boon to the community's women, whose health is often neglected. The health centre also doubles as a vocational training institute in the afternoon, at which women are taught income-generation skills such as tailoring. Sushil has been a strong supporter of Shanti Sahyog, which is run by a dedicated team headed by an ardent Gandhian, Suman Khanna Agarwal, an Associate Professor of Philosophy at the University of Delhi "I was happy when Sushil visited our adopted slum Sudhar Camp in Kalkaji to acquaint himself first-hand with our Slum Community Development Projects and interact with our Play/Pre School slum children. About five thousand patients annually benefit from the free Health Centre we run funded by him. He also sponsors our annual Eye Camp wherein almost 400 slum dwellers gain access to a free eye-check up, free spectacles and cataract operations," she says. She further adds that Sushil is a compassionate human being, and a great humanitarian with a missionary zeal to serve the underprivileged.

The Ila Trust, headed by Ritaji, is another Delhi institution dedicated to providing medical care to underprivileged communities. It has three vans – mobile clinics – that travel from the lanes of Chandni Chowk in Old Delhi to the slums of New Delhi, treating about 300 patients daily. The Ansals have paid for one of these vans and regularly help the Ila Trust with financial support that meets part of the expenses for the doctors' salaries and medicines. "The devoted doctors of mobile clinics who go to GB Road and treat HIV patients on a regular basis are doing an immense service," says Sushil.

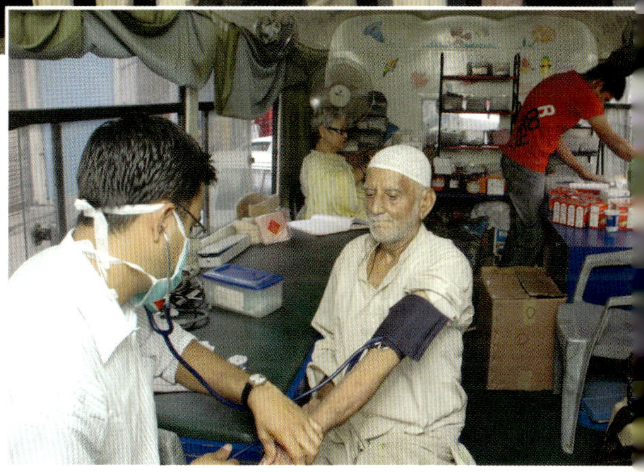

Sushil is determined that the proposed Sushil Ansal Foundation – like the Chiranjiv Charitable Trust – must be financially independent of individual influence as well as corporate fluctuations. The board of directors of Ansal API, on Sushil's request, has agreed to set aside up to 0.5 per cent of the company's profit every year for CSR purposes. At its discretion, the board can increase the contribution in a specific year. Sushil himself and individual members of the family also put in extra. That aside, the Sushil Foundation will earn regular rental income from two commercial flats and earn interest from some bank deposits. In addition, the Chiranjiv Charitable Trust already has properties and assets worth over Rs. 100 crores to its name. The regular income from these is used by the Trust for its many social welfare activities.

Kusum and Sushil have also supported literary activities for decades now, encouraging Hindi writers by sponsoring a literary society called Samvad. As a writer herself, Kusum has been instrumental managing it. This engagement is being taken further with the setting up of the Kusumanjali Foundation for Literature, Art and Culture. Indeed, Kusum and Sushil hope the rest of their years will be kept busy by the

HEALTH ON WHEELS
The Ila Foundation is a mobile clinic that travels to some of Delhi's humblest areas and is backed by the Sushil Ansal Foundation

twin foundations. Sushil puts it pithily, "As age is advancing, I feel I must pay back more and more to society."

This is a man who has paid his dues many times over but never once forgotten where he's come from. It's fitting then that the last mile of the Sushil's saga must take us to Kahma, the little village in Nawashahr District, Jalandar, where the Ansals started their journey. In 1975, Sushil and his father opened a hospital in Kahma. Today the Hansraj Government Hospital – named for Sushil's grandfather – serves the village and many surrounding ones as well. Every November, the Ansals organise a free eye camp at the hospital and this is when the family tries to visit. When Kusum went to Kahma for the first time, she was touched by the reception. "There was so much goodwill," she remembers, "I was treated as the daughter-in-law of the village." The Kahma Welfare Committee, an NGO that the Ansals have incubated, is now building a computer education centre that will have special facilities for female students. Shri Taman Singh, dynamic General Secretary of Kamha

Welfare Committee says "Kamha village and its neighbouring villages are highly grateful to Sushilji and Lalaji (Sushi's father) for donating Hansraj Government Hospital and for continuously giving financial assistance to meet the expenses of doctors, medicines and annual health check-up/ eye camps on regular basis. Their soul and spirit still throbs in the village and surrounding areas."

The hospital has been built on the agricultural land that was once all that the Ansals owned. "My grandfather had sugarcane fields," Sushil says, dipping into stories he has heard, "he used to harvest the crop, make gur [jaggery] and then sell it in his little shop." It was a small village and a simple life. Sushil runs a business empire that is exponentially larger and lives in a city much bigger than Kahma can imagine. Yet, somehow, that simplicity has never left him. To his friends and well-wishers, the sweet taste of the jaggery his ancestors sold defines him. As he learnt from his father, human service is the best of all prayers, and it still runs in his veins.

Facing Page

CULTURE OF GIVING:

A Senior Citizens' Home – or home away from home where they are cared for and kept happy and healthy.

Above

NURTURING THE ROOTS

Sushil donated a hospital to Kahma Village in the name of his grandfather Hansraj. It is being supported by the Sushil Ansal Foundation.

MANY "FIRSTS" ATTRIBUTABLE TO SUSHIL ANSAL, CHAIRMAN, ANSAL API

FIRST TO INTRODUCE THE **CONCEPT OF HIGH-RISE OFFICE BUILDINGS** IN DELHI – BUILT THE FIRST HIGH-RISE BUILDING, **AKASH DEEP,** AT BARAKHAMBA ROAD, CONNAUGHT PLACE, NEW DELHI, IN THE YEAR 1969, ON OWNERSHIP BASIS, FOLLOWED BY SEVERAL OTHER HIGH-RISES LIKE SURYA KIRAN, ANSAL BHAWAN, ANTRIKSH BHAWAN, INDRAPRAKASH, PRABHAT KIRAN, STATESMAN HOUSE AND TOLSTOY HOUSE, CHANGING THE SKYLINE OF DELHI.

FIRST TO MAKE THE **RESIDENTIAL APARTMENT BUILDING, ASHA DEEP,** ON OWNERSHIP BASIS AT HAILEY ROAD, CONNAUGHT PLACE, NEW DELHI IN THE YEAR 1971.

FIRST TO BUILD **VIKAS MINAR**, THE TALLEST BUILDING IN DELHI, COMPLETED FOR THE DDA IN THE YEAR 1975.

SUCCESSFULLY COMPLETED SEVERAL CONSTRUCTION CONTRACTS IN **IRAQ, RUSSIA AND BANGLADESH** BETWEEN 1979 AND 1990.

FIRST TO START THE CONCEPT OF SELLING **BUILT-UP VILLAS AND HOMES** IN TOWNSHIPS RATHER THAN JUST DEVELOP PLOTS IN PALAM VIHAR, GURGAON IN 1982.

FIRST TO BUILD A REVOLVING RESTAURANT, **PARIKRAMA,** LOCATED IN THE HEART OF DELHI AT ANTRIKSH BHAWAN, KASTURBA GANDHI MARG IN THE YEAR 1989.

FIRST DEVELOPER TO RECEIVE RBI CLEARANCE TO INVEST AND EXECUTE REAL-ESTATE PROJECTS LIKE CONDOMINIUM BUILDINGS AND SERVICE APARTMENTS IN **THAILAND** IN 1989 AND LATER IN **VIETNAM & NEPAL.**

ONE OF THE FIRST REAL ESTATE COMPANIES TO GET LISTED IN THE **STOCK EXCHANGES** OF MUMBAI AND DELHI IN THE YEAR 1992.

FIRST TO PIONEER AND FACILITATE THE CONSTRUCTION OF MULTIPLEX CULTURE IN THE CAPITAL AND N.C.R. BY BUILDING THE FIRST MULTIPLEX, **ANUPAM PVR,** (NOW KNOWN AS PVR) IN SAKET, IN THE YEAR 1996.

FIRST TO BRING IN THE CONCEPT OF A SHOPPING MALL, **ANSAL PLAZA,** IN DELHI, IN THE YEAR 1998, FOLLOWED BY A CHAIN OF MALLS WITH THE BRAND NAME OF ANSAL PLAZA IN HARYANA, PUNJAB, U.P. AND RAJASTHAN.

ONE OF THE FIRST ORGANIZED DEVELOPERS TO GO TO **TIER-II CITIES** LIKE SONEPAT IN HARYANA IN THE YEAR 2003, FOLLOWED BY PANIPAT, KARNAL, KURUKSHETRA AND SEVERAL CITIES IN PUNJAB, RAJASTHAN AND U.P.

FIRST TO HAND OVER COMPLETED HOMES AND PLOTS IN THE AMBITIOUS **HI-TECH TOWNSHIPS** IN U.P. IN THE YEAR 2009.

PHASE SEVEN

NEW FRONTIERS

MODEL TOWNS
Aquapolis, Ghaziabad, on the left and Sushant Golf City, Lucknow, on the right, are future models of the Ansal brand

Having turned seventy in November 2009, Sushil has been talking of slowing down. Even so, given his hectic schedule, with constant travel and a stream of business meetings every day, it is best to be somewhat sceptical about the supposedly imminent retirement. Retirement and slowing down are emotional decisions, usually impossible to quantify or measure in tangible terms. Yet, some numbers from the history of Ansal API merit iteration. In the years it has been around, the Ansal group of companies have constructed or developed about 400 million square feet across India, largely in the north – in Delhi and neighbouring states such as Haryana, Uttar Pradesh, Rajasthan and Punjab – but also in other parts of the country like Maharashtra, Madhya Pradesh, Karnataka and Kerala. In addition, Sushil's overseas ventures have resulted in the creation of 3.57 million square feet of residential and commercial space in Iraq, Thailand and Russia.

The statistics sound impressive and speak of a lifetime of labour. Yet, it is sobering to consider that Sushil, Pranav and their company have just embarked on a project called Sushant Golf City, initially spread across 3,500 acres in Lucknow, with a built up area of 180 million square feet and valued at Rs 20,000 crore. This is likely to be expanded to 6,000 acres, with a built up area of 270 million square feet. It is already being nicknamed "New Lucknow". In NCR, Sushil is conceptualising an even more ambitious project: Megapolis. Located in Dadri (adjoining Greater Noida), an hour's drive from Delhi, the first phase of Megapolis will extend to 2,500 acres and will have a built up area of 124 million square feet, with a value of approximately Rs 35,000 crore. Sushil plans to expand Megapolis to 5,000 acres as well.

Sushant Golf City and Megapolis represent the largest and most expansive property development projects ever undertaken by Sushil. Even individually, in sheer scale they dwarf the

REIMAGINING AVADH'S GRANDEUR

Ansal projects in Lucknow

Business
international
ansal API

MEGA WORKPLACES

Proposed corporate park at Megapolis, a township of 2,500 acres

entire construction record of Ansal API and its predecessor companies over the past four decades. Quite obviously, a man moving into such challenging territory cannot seriously claim to be contemplating retirement. Sushil laughs away the charge and insists his job is only to get the new townships rolling, to finalize the blueprints. The actual implementation and the end product will be in the hands of a future generation. "The Dadri and Lucknow projects will take fifteen years to complete," Sushil says, "frankly, they are for Pranav and Ayush [Pranav's son] and for our team of senior and dedicated professionals to handle." Indeed, on some recent trips to Lucknow, Sushil took along fourteen-year-old Ayush for site visits. Ayush was inquisitive and asked several questions about the project, just as Sushil

Above
NEXT IN LINE:
It is fitting that Sushil is beginning projects that Pranav will eventually bring to fruition

Facing page
THREE GENERATIONS
with Pranav and his son Ayush

used to do when he used to accompany his father to construction sites while still a schoolboy.

Megapolis and Sushant Golf City are more than extraordinarily sized projects for Sushil. Perhaps because of the juncture at which they have come, at the close of a period of tribulations, he has enormous emotional investment in them. They are his benediction to Pranav – as both father and group helmsman he is very conscious that he needs to give his son and successor a vast canvas, untainted by memories of family disputes or the Uphaar tragedy. Of course, it is for Pranav to paint the canvas, and he has decades to do that. Daughter-in-law Sheetal acknowledges the richness of this legacy: "He is a visionary. The land banks he has built are awesome. Even without further acquisitions, they can keep the group busy for twenty years."

In some respects, Megapolis and Sushant Golf City also represent a fulfilment of Sushil's dreams and address many of the frustrations of his career. For the first time, he has control of a vast, seemingly limitless and contiguous area and is free to design it his way, within the broad parameters of the Uttar Pradesh government's Hi-Tech Policy. He is building, not individual apartment blocks or even large neighbourhoods but, really, two cities. No more is he hamstrung by municipal busybodies and bureaucrats; he is free to imagine and shape an urban space as he would want. The misgivings of the early years, the anger at the manner in which the DDA made a mess of, for example, Nehru Place in Delhi, by erecting soulless office towers without leisure or recreation facilities or even adequate parking, the disappointment that the government agencies in Gurgaon did not build the roads, sewer lines and external infrastructure to complement the impressive commercial complexes and residential colonies put in place by private developers – Sushil can now overcome all of those. "In Gurgaon, we built high-rises and people moved in," he says, "and it was only after that that the government brought municipal services and external infrastructure to connect the internal facilities provided by the developers. It is unfortunate that Gurgaon is facing acute infrastructure bottlenecks which affect the quality of life for its residents."

In Megapolis and Sushant Golf City this will not be repeated. Sushil and his colleagues are going to ensure that internal and external services and social infrastructure, like schools and clubs and hospitals, as well as safety mechanisms, are in place even before the first resident arrives. "If nothing else, the customer expectation and competition will ensure that we keep to our word," he says. Ansal API has to not only build the houses, it has to take care of the internal roads, the power supply and garbage collection, it has to make the cities viable as places of residence, work and leisure for those who live there. It's the opportunity Sushil Ansal has been waiting for all his life. Simultaneously, the projects also give him room to marry his professional demands to his larger social calling. Corporate social responsibility – or simply charity, as it was once termed – has been a constant companion through Sushil's career. This philosophy has been combined with the needs of the community that he hopes will one day make Megapolis and Sushant Golf City its home, and Sushil has tailored some of his social sector initiatives to that. To understand what keeps Sushil busy these days, it is necessary to navigate with him the route map drawn for the two cities that have become his passion.

THE FUTURE
Model of Sushant Golf City, Lucknow on over 4,000 acres with a buildable area of 120 million square feet

FOR A NEW CENTURY

Model of Megapolis, near Greater Noida on 2,500 acres with a buildable area of 80 million square feet.

Both Megapolis and Sushant Golf City are benchmarked against international standards. The master plans have been drawn up by a well-known firm of architects – Woodhams, Meikle and Zhan – based in Auckland, New Zealand. "We are conscious that we are developing cities that should seem modern and contemporary in the latter part of the twenty-first century," says Sushil. "Two firms of landscapists and environmental architects, KTGY Inter Associates and PL Design, have come down from Thailand to help us with parks, lakes, fountains and forests and to make the cities eco-friendly, less environmentally- and sound-polluted. You will be surprised at the time and effort being spent on developing a uniform signage system that is both aesthetic and utilitarian."

This is a very different game and Sushil clearly loves it. As he says, he is looking to build landmarks, not just rows of houses and office blocks but a refined urban consciousness. "This is what value addition is, this is real 'development'," he explains, "to build not just walls and floors but ensure a better quality of life for the people who will live in and use our townships. The master planning architectural controls, streetscapes,

THINKING BIG
Model of Aquapolis, Ghaziabad, which is presently being built

skylines, the right ambience and environment are now in our control. Whether a particular park will resemble a Japanese garden or a Mughal garden will be our decision. Local transport within the cities will be provided by us. We have taken a decision that the vehicles will be battery-operated or conform to the green fuel of the day."

Pragmatic to the last millimetre, Sushil realises building two cities simultaneously is a mammoth task for Ansal API. Passionate about business and particularly about encouraging younger entrepreneurs, he has devised a scheme for Sushant Golf City as well as Megapolis. "Conforming to our master design, a small entrepreneur, starting out in the property development field, can build and sell or lease out service apartments, clubs, malls, offices within our cities." Sushil says, "this is what the DDA told us to do with, say, Nehru Place, and I see this as my chance to give back."

Since the cities will have no municipalities for the foreseeable future, the Ansals will be responsible for civic management and physical infrastructure upkeep. Two companies – Star Estates Facilities Management and Ansal Infrastructure – have been promoted for this purpose. Their initial charter is to manage Ansal API's own cities as separate profit-making centres and become urban infrastructure service providers for other developers and municipal bodies as well. "In the larger reckoning," Sushil says, "the idea is to build and maintain world-class cities even outside our metros. That is where India's tomorrow lies. We can't be bottled up in a shortage economy mindset forever."

What will Sushil's cities look like? In Lucknow, a Medical City has been planned and will incorporate facilities from leading health-care institutions. Over 100 school sites have been identified. An Education City has been planned on 150 acres. The best national and international institutions of higher learning are being invited here. Branches of the Ansal Institute of Technology and of the Sushant School of Architecture will commence classes in 2012. A site for a Film and Media City has been set aside. Filmmaker Muzaffar Ali fell in love with the natural beauty of the location on a visit to Sushant Golf City and has agreed to help Sushil in nurturing this project. Says P.N. Mishra, executive director (business development) of Ansal API, "We have all worked with fervour in conceptualising Sushant Golf City. We are not only attempting to ensure a high quality of life to the future residents, we are actually building a city of our dreams."

SPECTACULAR LANDSCAPE
Illustration of the proposed The Palms, in Sushant Golf City, Lucknow

A healthy mind needs a healthy body, as Sushil sees it. Being a sportsperson from his school days, he is sad about the standard of sports and sports facilities in India. "It's a pity that a country of a billion people wins so few Olympic medals," he says, arguing that successful business houses must step in and redress this imbalance and invest in creating world-class training centres. With this in mind, Sushil is putting up a high tech, modern, multi-sport stadium complex over twenty acres of Sushant Golf City. It will be among the most impressive sports facilities developed in the private sector in India. It will also incorporate specialized sports academies in football, hockey, cricket, tennis, basketball, badminton, athletics and other sports. Residential facilities will also be available within the campus. The hope is to create Olympic winners and Wimbledon champions.

Separately, the British firm Martin Hawtree – "the world's longest continuous golf architectural practice", having been in the golf course design and construction business for a century – is supervising the creation of a spectacular golf course that will be the centrepiece of Sushant Golf City. A golfing community, living in villas and apartments overlooking the course, will give this New Lucknow its edge. It's quite an aspiration for a city that is not generally seen as a business hub or particularly known for big-ticket consumer spending. Nevertheless, with his experience in smaller cities, outside the metros, Sushil was convinced there was untapped potential in Lucknow. "I knew there was money," he says, "it was waiting for an investment outlet." Villas around the golf course were announced for close to Rs 3 crore each, high prices for the property market in Lucknow. Within days, the initial launch of Phase I was sold out. Sushil's instincts were proved right yet again.

From a cultural centre on the lines of Delhi's India Habitat Centre to The Palms Club – "I promise you, it will be the best club in

the city, no question," announces Sushil – to a forty-storeyed building crowned by a revolving restaurant and presiding over the City of Nawabs, the Ansals' Golf City will have its stand-out features. It will also host a seventy-acre super-speciality hospital complex as well as biotech and information technology parks. Lucknow is a hub of Indian biotech and excellent research and development institutions are already there. The synergy with Sushant Golf City is obvious. All these are not dreams. Actual deals have already been done. The Golf City will also house India's finest auto park, with showrooms and service facilities for all leading automobile companies. Wal Mart, the global retail giant, is setting up a massive cash-and-carry operation here, starting in 2011-12.

Sushant Golf City saw an important business innovation on the part of Sushil. One day, he invited the leading developers of Lucknow and neighbouring cities for lunch and made a video presentation on "New Lucknow." He urged them to join him as partners and collaborators and pick up residential, commercial or multiplex complexes, IT parks, biotech parks, schools, hospitals or any other project shown and approved in the scheme. Ansal API would facilitate all approvals and sanctions, including the design of the buildings, and would maintain architectural control to ensure planned and aesthetic development.

After the presentation Pavan Agarwal (R.R. Dwellings) and Alok Chandra (Chandra Modern Builders), two leading builders of Lucknow, walked up to Sushil and said that never before had a large developer come up with "this idea of inviting competitors to share his cake." The idea proved extremely successful. Within a span of one year, most of the leading developers and builders of Lucknow joined hands in one form or the other and became a part of the Sushant Golf City mission. Companies like Lakshya Real Infra, Tulsiani Constructions and Developers, Tuilp Buildwell and Rishita Developers and many others today are promoting the new city alongside Sushil and Pranav, all sharing a common dream.

The ambit for Megapolis is also exciting and challenging. Located on National Highway 91 and not too far from the Greater Noida-Agra Expressway, Megapolis will be only 25 kilometres from the proposed Taj Airport and Aviation Hub in Jewar (on the border of Bulandshahr and Aligarh district). This is envisaged as the Delhi metropolitan area's second international airport. A dedicated freight corridor and container depot/

dry port is coming up nearby. A Formula I race track is only a few kilometres away. Greater Noida and Dadri are blessed with prodigious groundwater. Five large lakes in the area of the Megapolis project are being developed as urban water bodies, with walkways and lakeside promenades.

Discussing the vision for Megapolis with Sushil, it is easy to believe he is indulging his fantasies. As a sportsman, he is particularly sold on cities with vast green expanses. Sushil has a polo ground and a world-class equestrian club in mind for Megapolis. There will also be that Ansal standard: the international tournament-ready golf course. The Megapolis course is being designed by Nick Faldo, one of golf's all-time greats. A short drive from it will be the Mahesh Bhupathi Tennis Academy, named for and run by a Wimbledon champion who no doubt hopes to find his successors. Covering a hundred acres, the medical city, a consortium of super-speciality hospitals, at Megapolis will be even larger than that in Lucknow. While the tallest building planned so far in Megapolis is the twenty-five-storey Crystal Towers, Sushil confesses to a secret desire: "If possible and if feasible, I would like Megapolis to have one of the tallest buildings in India."

To improve connectivity to Megapolis from Greater Noida, an over-bridge is being jointly developed by Ansal API and the Bulandshahr-Dadri Development Authority. Vinod Kumar Saigal, executive director (projects), Ansal API, says, "We chose this location because a perennial water canal flows through it. This provides an excellent opportunity to us to undertake waterfront development on the lines of Paris or Saint Petersburg. With Megapolis, we are setting our standards really high."

The Delhi Metro is being extended further to Badooki Railway Station, touching Megapolis. The extension is expected to be completed by 2011-12 and this connection will create a seamless National Capital Region mass transit system. In spite of this, Sushil is not looking at Megapolis as a city that will live off Delhi. He wants to create a self-contained urban ecosystem that will provide its residents and users avenues for living, working, leisure and education, have its own reference points, and be an autonomous city rather than a far-flung suburb of India's capital.

Both the Lucknow township and Megapolis will need enormous physical infrastructure and its proper maintenance and upkeep. The physical infrastructure provided to accommodate a population of over three lakhs on the proposed extended area of 6,000 acres at Sushant Golf

City, Lucknow would require approximately 450 megawatts of power to be generated or taken from the U.P. Vitran Nigam. The sewage treatment plant would treat about sixty million litres per day. The total road length in the area would be about 350 kilometres. Sewage lines, water lines and storm water lines would each approximate 500 kilometres for a total of 1,500 kilometres. Two railway under-bridges and a few canal bridges will be built to allow transport and movement within the area. The Megapolis when extended to 5,000 acres will be approximately 16 per cent smaller than Golf City; consequently the physical infrastructure will be reduced. These facilities will be maintained by Ansal's facility management company, which will have a challenging task ahead to ensure quality drinking water, sewage lines, uninterrupted power supply, etc.

Another project that Sushil is excited about is the mega luxury tourist project, a 75-minute drive from Delhi, in Gurgaon. An international standard link Golf Course popularly known as Golden Greens, designed by famous British designer Martin Hawtree, has already been operative for a few years. Sushil and Pranav have joined Rajender Miglani (Sheetal's father) to expand this complex to 300 acres and develop it jointly with him into a world-class tourist complex. The location, at the foot of the Aravalis, is most picturesque and scenic. "We plan to have about 300 beautiful golf villas, high-class luxurious condominiums, a five-star hotel and a rejuvenating spa. In addition to Golf Club, we would provide other sports and recreational facilities to make it an all inclusive family holiday and recreational destination," echo Rajender and Sushil, who share a common dream.

There is a fourth project keeping Sushil occupied these days. Esencia is located in Gurgaon, and at 110 acres is much smaller than Sushant Golf City and Megapolis. However, Sushil considers it equally if not more important. Esencia is India's first green township, registered as a pilot project under GRIHA (Green Rating and Integrated Habitat Assessment), a Government of India enterprise. This will be an eco-friendly neighbourhood, with minimum solid and water waste and recycling of treated effluents. Partnering Ansal API in Esencia is ADARSH (the Association of Development and Research of Sustainable Habitats), a body registered with the Indian Ministry of New and Renewable Energy and with TERI (The Energy and Resources Institute).

EARLY YEARS

Shining city: A night view of Megapolis

WEST PROMINADE SQUARE
GATE WAY TOWER
GATE WAY SQUARE
OAKWOOD EAST APARTMENTS 2
LEGACY OAKS SQUARE 4

On asking how his dreams will be fully realised, Sushil confidently points to his crew: "We have a very strong professional team led by Pranav (vice-chairman and managing director), ably assisted by Anil Kumar (joint managing director and CEO), Vijay Jindal (joint managing director), V.K. Saigal (executive director [projects]), Vinod Tikku (executive director [technical]), M.L. Soni, Rakesh Kaul, Surajit Roy, Shashank Jain, Subash Bansal, Amitav Ganguly, N.K. Sehgal, Vivek Gandhi, Lalit Rastogi, Raghunandan and a large number of other senior and dedicated executives. They will raise the bar continuously, and I am confident, will take Ansal API to greater heights, and contribute to the growth and development of the country."

Sushil firmly believes that high ethical standards must be practiced in business to win the trust and faith of business associates, collaborators, stakeholders and shareholders. Anil Kumar, Joint MD and CEO of Ansal API, says "we believe in rewarding our shareholders and are happy that, with the issue of bonus shares, right issues, splitting of shares and uninterrupted payment of dividends since our inception in 1992, we've given approximately 108 per cent return per annum to our shareholders."

Sushil continues, "to guide and ensure a high standard of corporate governance, we have highly motivated, respected, competent and independent directors on the board like Mr. D.N. Davar, Mr. R.C. Vaish, Mr. O.P. Mehra, Mr. P.R. Khanna and Mr. Lalit Bhasin, who are invaluable assets to the growth and development of the company."

Mr. D.N. Davar, an ex-Development Banking Chief, and a tremendous business acumen who has known Sushil for over twenty years and has been a Director of Board of Ansal API for over a decade says that " Sushil belongs to a rare genre of business visionaries combining astute corporate chief's traits of leadership and inspiring team work. He is a doyen in the real estate sector who has steadily built the formidable Ansal brand and earned respect and esteem in business circles."

As he discusses his plans, Sushil's eyes light up and the spark from those hot days and steaming nights in Hapur, half a century ago, comes alive again. More than anything else, it is that passion that keeps him going. It is rooted in the quest for excellence, in the belief that he must climb the highest mountain and serve the society that has given him so much – and in the conviction that his finest decade lies ahead of him.

AT PEACE WITH HIMSELF: *Sushil has always considered inner calm more important than external riches*

"RICHES ARE NOT FROM AN
ABUNDANCE OF WORLDLY GOODS,
BUT FROM A CONTENTED MIND"

Mohammed